No CARTOON LEFT BEHIND!

THE BEST OF ROB ROGERS

No CARTOON LEFT BEHIND !

THE BEST OF ROB ROGERS

Carnegie Mellon University Press

Pittsburgh 2009

This book was made possible with generous support from *The Pittsburgh Post-Gazette*, *Carnegie Mellon University* and *The American College of Chest Physicians*.

Book design by Paul Schifino, schifinodesign.com

Library of Congress Control Number 2009927664
ISBN 978-0-88748-515-2
Copyright © 2009 by Rob Rogers
All rights reserved
Printed and bound in China

10   9   8   7   6   5   4   3   2   1

FOR LINDA...

... a brilliant poet, fierce friend and beloved sister.
Your courage, lust for life and generous spirit still inspire me.
I miss laughing together at the things only we found funny.
The world is a sadder place without you in it,
but a better place for having known you.

Linda and Mojo in Venice Beach, 1994.

WITH A SPECIAL NOD TO MY "EVERYMAN"

Dad, you encouraged me to draw from the moment I could hold a crayon.

You were always proud of me, even if I was drawing you in an unflattering way.

Later, through your own artwork, you taught me that it's never too late to chase a dream.

I think about you every time I put pen to paper.

Whether I am drawing a butcher, a baker or a candlestick maker,

your spirit is always in there somewhere.

As long as I can draw, you will always be with me.

This was the cover art for the 50th anniversary convention of the Association of American Editorial Cartoonists held in Washington, D.C. in 2007.

PEEK-A-BOO!

TABLE OF CONTENTS

Part of the Strike Force after sneaking into a private party at the 2000 DNC in Los Angeles. Pictured from left to right are: Booger (Rob Rogers), Magenta Eagle (Dave Barry), Pocket Fisherman (Chip Bok) and Sourdough (Mayor Riordan). Pocket Fisherman later admitted he got the phone cord stuck in his ear and it didn't come out until the next morning.

FOREWORD

Rob Rogers is a deranged cartoonist.

Wait, that's redundant.

Rob Rogers is a cartoonist. I have the privilege of knowing a number of cartoonists, and they are fine, fun-loving people, but they tend to be a few forks short of a fondue set. The reason they became cartoonists in the first place is that they're free spirits who are not suited to professions that impose harsh restrictions, such as keeping regular hours, answering the telephone, or having to wear clothes.

I've been a fan of Rob Rogers' work for many years. His cartoons are funny, hard-hitting, and brilliantly drawn, as you'll see when you page through this excellent book. But Rob is more than just a gifted cartoonist. He is also a good man to have on your side in a tight situation. I learned this when I first got to know Rob personally, back in 2000, when he and I both covered the Republican and Democratic national political conventions. Rob and I became part of a Strike Force of a half-dozen or so guys—all cartoonists except for me— who expended a tremendous amount of time and effort performing the most critical mission of the news media at political conventions; namely, trying to get into parties to which we were not invited. It's hard, thankless work, but somebody has to do it.

Our high point, as a Strike Force, occurred during the Democratic National Convention in Los Angeles. There was this really hot exclusive party being thrown by a powerful lobbying firm. Everybody wanted to go, but invitations were very hard to get.

As it happened, on the morning of the party, I had a breakfast meeting with the mayor of Los Angeles, a man named Dick "Dick" Riordan, who had agreed (I am not making this up) to endorse me for president. Since I wanted to look presidential, I asked Rob Rogers and the rest of the Strike Force members if they would serve as my Secret Service agents. Naturally, being professional cartoonists, they agreed. They arrived at the meeting wearing suits and sunglasses, and they had cords stuck into their ears and running down into their suit jackets. These cords were taken from hotel telephones (Rob's brilliant idea), so they didn't actually do anything. But they looked official.

So anyway, after Mayor Dick endorsed me for president, we all got to talking, and he revealed that he would be attending the exclusive party that night. At this point, you could actually see the light bulb turn on over the collective heads of the Strike Force. We asked Mayor Dick if we could serve as his security detail at the party. And Mayor Dick—in one of the most courageous and decisive decisions I have ever seen a public official make— immediately said yes.

That night the Strike Force gathered in the parking lot of the swank restaurant where the exclusive party was being held. We all had our telephone ear cords in our ears, and we all wore our dark suits and sunglasses, even though it was, technically, night. We also, for security purposes, gave ourselves secret code names. Mine was "Magenta Eagle." Rob's was "Booger."

So there we were, in the parking lot, milling around in our sunglasses and reviewing various aspects of the security operation. ("What's my secret code name again?") We must have looked fairly suspicious, because the security people hired for the party were giving us the eyeball. But just when it looked as though they might call the police, Mayor Dick (whom we had given the secret code name "Sourdough") showed up with his wife ("Pork Chop") and motioned to us to accompany him into the party, and since he was the actual mayor of the actual city, they had to let us in.

Once we got inside, we immediately executed our two-prong security plan, as follows:

PRONG ONE — Wave goodbye to Mayor Sourdough and Pork Chop.

PRONG TWO — Head for the bar.

After that, my memory of the evening is hazy, but as far as I know nobody was killed or anything. So I chalk it up as another highly successful Strike Force operation. And it would not have been possible without the dedication and hard work of Rob Rogers.

My point is this: You may think, as you look through the cartoons in this book, that Rob Rogers has a cushy job. You may think that being a professional cartoonist is just a matter of thinking up a joke and drawing a goofy picture. But you are wrong. Often you have to think up a joke and draw a goofy picture while hung over. So cut the man some slack. Remember that, while you're at home at night with your family, safe and secure, Rob Rogers might be out engaged in some kind of treacherous journalism operation, with a very real risk that he will wind up in a hospital emergency room having a hotel phone cord removed from his ear.

There is no need to thank him: He's just doing his job.

— Dave Barry

INTRODUCTION

Hockey player meets rodeo clown.

That's how I would best describe the job I do. Some days I am checking politicians against the boards hard enough to make them organ donors. Other days it's my job to step into an otherwise tragic environment wearing baggy pants, a red nose and giant clown shoes.

In hockey there are certain physical players who are designated as "enforcers" and it is their job to pick fights and mix it up on the ice. While editorials and opinion columns use calm and measured arguments to score points, I skate in and try to knock some sense into the opposing team. We all know that old joke about going to a boxing match and seeing a hockey game break out. Well, I have never heard the expression, "I went to a hockey game and a civil discussion of the issues broke out."

In a rodeo, mortal men and women willingly enter an arena and allow their fragile bodies to be flung around by giant brutal beasts. It is not unlike voters who elect leaders they know will abuse them. As the rodeo clown, I try to give the readers a laugh so they won't think about the bull crushing their ribs.

While I try to approach each topic on its own merits, anyone familiar with my work knows my politics fall into the "liberal" category. Editorial cartoonists are like visual op-ed columnists. They express their own opinion on pages designed to house a variety of opinions. There are liberal cartoonists and conservative cartoonists. Nobody would expect George Will to take a liberal viewpoint. He's a conservative columnist who gets paid to express his conservative view. Yet I receive calls and letters all the time asking why I don't draw something with a more conservative bent.

This book was a true labor of love. I spent four years off-and-on putting it together. Now you know what happens to me when I don't have a hard deadline (someday I will finish my book, *You Too Can Moonwalk Like Michael Jackson!*) After finishing a section, I would realize that several months had gone by and I needed to add the cartoons I had completed during that time. I have drawn roughly 240 cartoons a year for the past 25 years. That's 6,000 cartoons! Despite the title of the book, some of those cartoons had to be left behind. It is a cliché to say that my cartoons are like children to me, but then, cartoonists are known for using clichés (the newspaper doesn't receive as many nasty letters about actual children.) Each chapter became my own personal *Sophie's Choice*, having to decide which child to take and which one to leave behind. Don't cry my little "Bush-As-A-Pilgrim-Pardoning-The-Iraq-War-Rationale-Turkey." Your brother, "Bush-As-Lord-Of-The-Wedding-Ring-Golem" and I will see you again some day soon (sniff, sniff).

When I tell people I am an editorial cartoonist, I get one of three standard responses. It is either, "I don't read the paper," or "how do you come up with something every day?" or the not-so-flattering, "what else do you do?" Contrary to what some readers might believe, I work a full day. I spend several hours a day reading newspapers, writing down topics and working out ideas in my sketchbook. Then I spend the rest of the day executing the final drawing.

I like it when readers vent about my cartoons. If they weren't calling and writing letters to the editor I would wonder if I was slipping. I once received a call from a reader who complained about a comparison I made between Hiroshima and terrorism. I spent twenty minutes on the phone with him explaining, as sensitively and intelligently as I could, what I was trying to say in the cartoon. He dismissively said, "I don't agree, and as long as I have you on the phone, I want to complain about another cartoon you drew. What kind of idiot would depict our president as a monkey?"

It isn't brain surgery or rocket science. I'm not saving the world one cartoon at a time. But I love my job. I love to get out of bed and go to work every day. (OK, the getting out of bed part isn't fun.) I get to spend my day filling a rectangular box with my opinion, humor and caricatures of newsworthy people (occasionally as a monkey). Some days I hope to be poignant. Other days I just hope to be funny. The best days are when I can be both.

That doesn't mean it isn't hard work. It doesn't mean I don't have days when I struggle to come up with an idea. And it doesn't mean I take my soapbox for granted. I never do. Whether I wake up as a hockey player or a rodeo clown, it never gets old. It is great work if you can get it. Unfortunately, with the slow but steady demise of the newspaper industry, it is fast becoming work you can't "get" anymore. Some days I feel like a VCR repairman. I don't care what the guys at Best Buy tell you — keep buying those VCRs!

— Rob Rogers

PART I

Finding My Inner Cartoonist

ABOVE: Rob, in 1965, preparing for a career that involves editors looking over his shoulder.

1 SNOOPY FORGER

THE EARLY YEARS

ABOVE: At age 10 I was fascinated by vultures, which explains why now I enjoy drawing politicians and corporate CEOs.

BELOW RIGHT: If you look close at the end of the bronchoscope you can spot a dog bone. I am not sure why it would be in his lung ... but at least that part wasn't forged.

My parents recognized my unique talent at an early age. Unfortunately, it was a talent for sticking Cheerios up my nose, which limited my career options. Needless to say, mom and dad were worried. Eventually, I became bored with breakfast cereals and traded them in for crayons. Wanting to expose me to culture, while saving money on a babysitter, my parents enrolled me in Saturday art classes at the museum. It soon became evident that I had a talent for art, which also limited my career options. Mom and dad were still worried.

My favorite comic strip growing up was *Peanuts*. I practiced mimicking Charles Schultz's drawing style until I could draw Snoopy without even looking. I even copied the *Peanuts* characters for my father's medical talks. He was a pulmonary physician (lungs). In one cartoon I show Snoopy having a bronchoscopy performed on him. That's where a telescopic tube is stuck up a patient's nose (again with things up the nose) and into their lungs to give the doctors a closer look. I drew it before I understood copyright law, of course. Sorry, Sparky.

At age 6, it was already clear I was watching too much Woody Woodpecker.

ROB THE CARTOONIST

I realized early on that drawing was only half the fun. I also wanted to write the scripts for my characters. By the age of 8 I was keeping a little black notebook of my cartoon stories. Looking back, I noticed a pattern emerging in the titles of these epic dramas. Clearly, they all needed to be about courageous men with gainful employment. Each title included a proper name followed by a profession. There was "Bob the Barber," "Jim the Skin Diver" and "Smithy the Cave Man," to name a few. Smithy the Cave Man? Sounds more like the name of an English butler than a Neanderthal. Oh, well. Each story showed these men overcoming incredible odds to conquer the likes of crooks, sharks and dinosaurs. How appropriate, then, that I would end up gainfully employed (Rob the Cartoonist) drawing cartoons about political crooks, sharks and dinosaurs. My little league baseball team was actually sponsored by Bob's Barber Shop. I had a friend named Jim. I am not sure where I got "Smithy." Maybe it was the championship game we played against the "Smithy's Bail Bonds" team.

ABOVE: *Bob the Barber* (circa 1967).

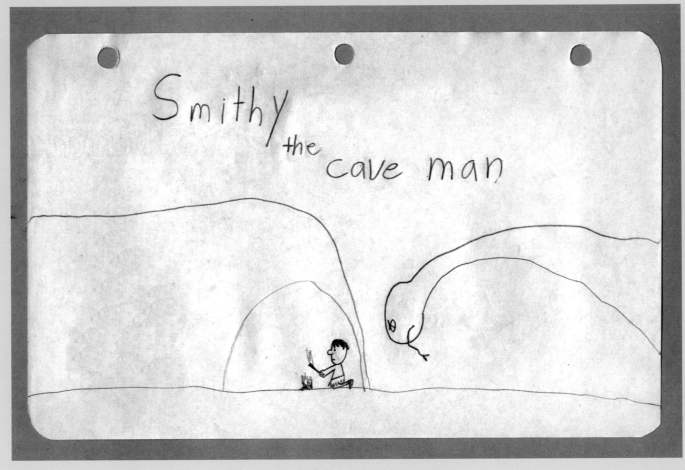

ABOVE: *Smithy the Cave Man* (circa 1967).

BELOW: *Jim the Skin Diver* (circa 1967).

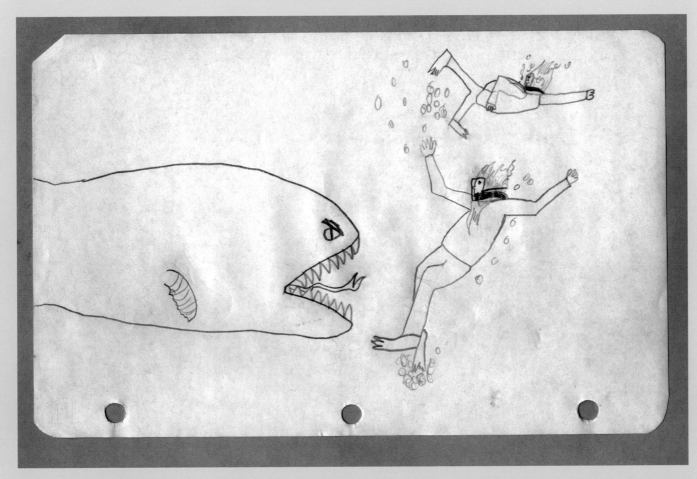

ABOVE: Rob at age 7.

5TH GRADE MONSTERS

In fifth grade I drew a series of monsters for a show-and-tell project about our hobbies. I remember standing up in front of the entire class, the lights dimmed, describing each monster in detail as I projected them using an opaque projector. When the presentation was over it dawned on me that people must think I'm a freak who sits around drawing monsters all day. Why couldn't I have had a normal hobby like Tommy Evans who collected Indian head nickels? Now when I give speeches I still dim the lights and show drawings of assorted monsters ... er, I mean elected officials. If I manage to get a few laughs from the audience I no longer regret my lack of Indian head nickels.

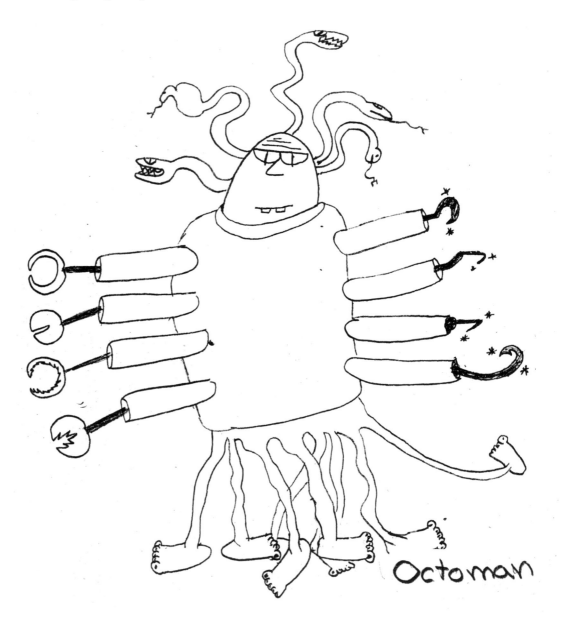

ABOVE: *Twins* (circa 1969).

RIGHT: *Octoman* (circa 1969).

OPPOSITE PAGE: *Metal Man* (circa 1969).

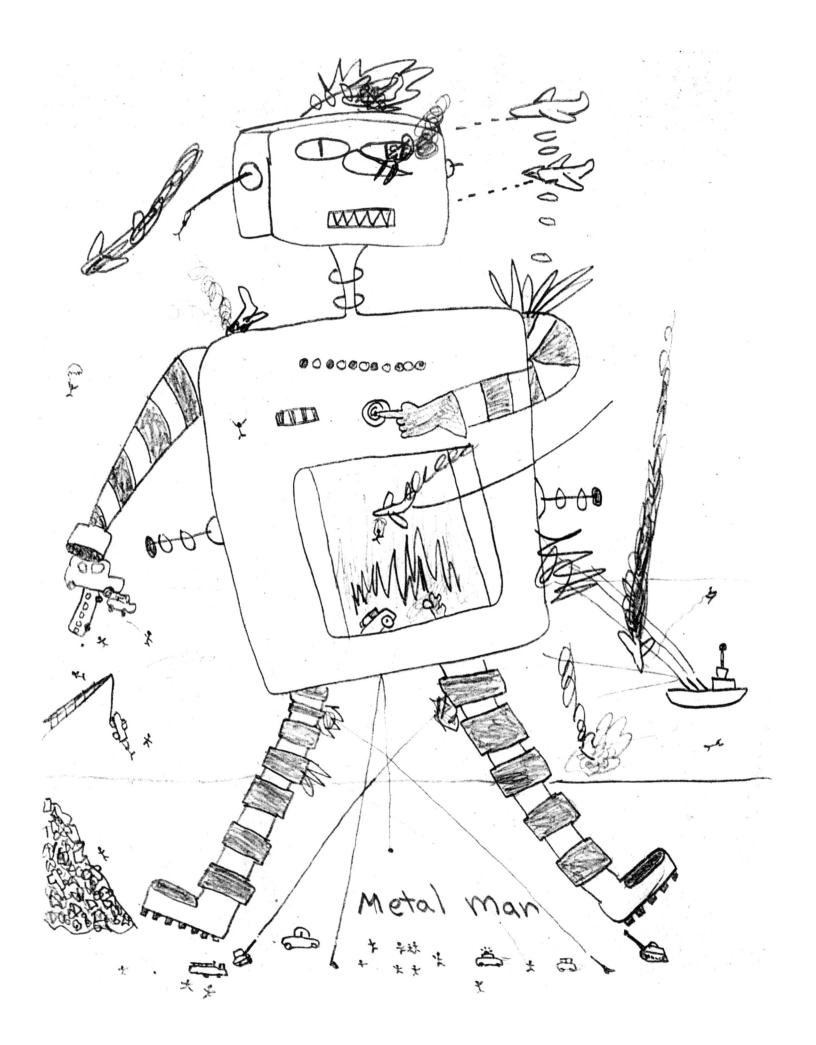

Metal man

MY DAD THE LUNG WASHER

When I was 10 I drew what I consider to be my first editorial cartoon. One night I saw my dad sorting slides for one of his medical talks and I asked him what he was doing. He explained to me how he helped perfect a treatment called "lung lavage" where saline was used to wash out a patient's lungs. The treatment is still used today to help patients with a rare form of lung disease. In his lecture he planned to show lots of boring charts and graphs to support his research. I figured he would need something to help keep the audience awake. I went upstairs and found his Gray's anatomy book to find a picture of some lungs. I titled the drawing "My Dad the Lung Washer." It showed my father scrubbing lungs with an old washboard and then hanging them on a clothesline to dry. My spelling was just as good back then as it is now (I still sometimes spell "lungwhasher" with two "H"s.) The best part? My dad had a full head of hair then and yet I chose to draw him completely bald. It probably had something to do with the time he wouldn't buy me that Stingray bike with the banana seat. Even at age 10 my pen was aimed at those in power.

My dad, the follicly challenged lung washer.

2 I WAS A TEENAGE McGOVERNIK

I'VE NEVER BEEN TO NAM BUT I'VE BEEN TO OKLAHOMA

Several things happened in 1972 that made a career in cartooning seem inevitable. First, I moved from Philadelphia to Oklahoma where the average eighth grader was 6′2″, 250 pounds, with an appetite for red meat. My lifelong dream of playing professional football was quickly crushed along with my spinal cord. I knew I would need another career track. Second, I discovered that drawing cartoons was a great way to impress girls. Of course, I was too shy to say anything to them ("he's nice for a mute cartoonist") but it was still pretty cool … especially since my plan to impress them on the football field had gone bust. Third, in my civics class we had an election-year project that included creating mock campaigns for Nixon and McGovern. I chose McGovern and thus began my tradition of supporting earnest, peace-loving liberals with no chance of winning.

Despite McGovern's devastating loss, the election left an imprint on me. I discovered that politics didn't have to be dead boring just because my father liked it. Then came Watergate. I felt vindicated that I had supported the non-crook. Politics stayed with me but I don't think I realized I could draw about politics for a living. My dream back then was to work for *Mad* Magazine. I was a huge Jack Davis fan. To kids like me the illustrators at *Mad* were like the Beatles. Jack Davis was my John Lennon. In my senior year in high school I won a $500 college art scholarship with a portfolio of Jack Davis-influenced cartoons (i.e., rip-offs). Please don't sue me, Jack.

My failure to make the baseball or football team (and believe me I tried) didn't mean I couldn't draw sports (circa 1975).

COW COLLEGE

We were living in the Philadelphia suburb of Swarthmore, home to the liberal Swarthmore College, when my dad got the job offer in Oklahoma. Talk about culture shock. I went from the bastion of liberalism to the bastion of cowboyism. During my freshman year at Oklahoma State University, I began to draw cartoons for the campus paper. My first cartoon made fun of a debate over whether new lights would make the campus pond safer for students or simply ruin the romantic ambience (in retrospect the cartoon was a bit insensitive to the fears and concerns of the female students, but hey, I was young and it was Oklahoma.) The cartoon generated letters and phone calls on both sides of the issue. "Wow," I thought, "all because of a little cartoon ... this is awesome!" A political cartoonist was born.

In the spring of 1979, midway through my sophomore year, I transferred to a smaller school, the University of Central Oklahoma, in hopes of getting more personal attention (from the cheerleaders.) My biggest artistic influence at the time was Jeff MacNelly, political cartoonist for the *Chicago Tribune* and creator of the comic strip *Shoe*. I was so enamored by his work I paid for a subscription to his newspaper so I could see his cartoons every day. Since Edmond, Oklahoma, was a bit outside of his paper's circulation area, the paper was mailed to me from Virginia. I can guarantee you I was the only person in the city

ABOVE LEFT: I was also a big David Levine fan. This caricature of Jimmy Carter was drawn in his style.

BELOW: Jimmy Carter suggested using women in the military but it didn't look like they would find equality there either. This was drawn for UCO's student paper called *The Vista*.

THETA POND NOW . . .

. . . AND LATER WITH NEW CRIME-PROOF LIGHTS

My very first published political cartoon was printed in Oklahoma State University's student paper,
The Daily O'Collegian, in 1977. They paid me ten bucks.

(and probably the state) reading a week-old copy of the *Richmond News-Leader* with my morning coffee. I checked out his first book, *MacNelly, the Pulitzer Winning Cartoonist*, from UCO's library and carried it around in my backpack like a bible (it was, after all, the Bible Belt). I studied the book until I had memorized every crosshatch on every page. I kept checking it out of the library over and over until the librarian finally told me I would have to leave it there for someone else to check out. Two weeks later I came back and checked it out again. The librarian just laughed. A few years ago I went back to UCO to receive an award. Believe it or not, the book was still there! It looked exactly the same including an ink stain that I accidentally applied to the cover while working on one of my college cartoons. The librarian working that day was so touched by my story she agreed to report the book "lost." It now sits proudly on my shelf.

MacNelly's influence is evident in this cartoon I drew during my final semester of graduate school in 1984.

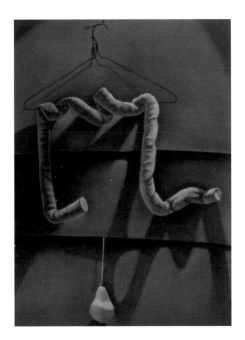

My grad school paintings of fabricated still
lifes showed no signs of an interest in political
cartooning (1982).

BACK TO THE BLUE STATE

Somehow I managed to make it back to Pennsylvania for graduate school. During my two-
year MFA program at Carnegie Mellon University I never told my professors I was a cartoonist. I was afraid they wouldn't take me seriously as a painter. During the opening of my
master's show I confessed to one of my professors that after graduation I would be starting
an editorial cartooning internship at the *Pittsburgh Press*. He looked at me like I had just told
him he was my real father. He stood there, eyes wide, too shocked to speak. It was either
because he felt that the last two years he'd spent pouring his heart and soul into me had
been a lie, or because he couldn't believe I had actually snagged a paying job as an artist.

The Pittsburgh Press   Wednesday, May 16, 1984

OPINION

ROGERS PITTSBURGH PRESS '84

NOW OPEN

IGHLAND PARK ZOO
ANIMAL HABITAT

"I KNEW THE EXTRA SPACE WOULD COME IN HANDY."

EM
litor

ROSS
ditor

BAUMANN
ing Editor/Graphics

. BROWN
anaging Editor/Sports

IAB
anaging Editor/News

HRENSKY
e Editor

luct the enroll-
tery system, a
the support of

My first cartoon as an intern at *The Pittsburgh Press* was published on May 16,
1984. I combined the ongoing problem of prison overcrowding with the opening
of the new zoo. In August of that year I was hired as a full-time cartoonist.

ALL POLITICS IS LOCAL

Not only do I have the privilege of working in my home state of Pennsylvania but I also get to draw cartoons about the sports-watching, union-loving, beer-drinking, pierogi-eating, people who inhabit the great Steel City of Pittsburgh. In my local weekly comic strip, "Brewed On Grant," local politicians and assorted others stop in to a fictitious diner on Grant Street to chat with Rosie the waitress. Grant Street houses the Mayor's office, council chambers, the county courthouse, row offices, etc. Here are a few recent examples.

In Pennsylvania you still can't buy liquor in a grocery store. The prohibition-era Liquor Control Board (LCB) continues to monopolize liquor sales. In 2003 the state decided to keep the LCB stores open on Sunday. At the same time, they cut funding that kept public libraries open on Sunday. *Published 07/23/03.*

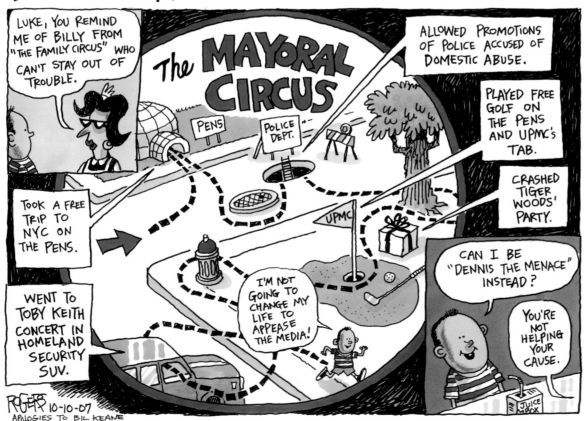

I like to draw Luke Ravenstahl, Pittsburgh's young mayor, as a petulant little boy drinking from a juice box. He had trouble staying out of the headlines his first year in office. It reminded me of the famous Bil Keane cartoon. *Published 10/10/07.*

Pittsburgh received some good press from national publications around the same time the infamous Obama fist-bump cartoon appeared on the cover of *The New Yorker*. For you non-locals, "Yinzer" is a term for a true Pittsburgher. "Yinz" is the Pittsburghese equivalent of "you all" or "yous guys."
Published 07/23/08.

When the Pittsburgh Steelers won a record-breaking sixth Super Bowl in 2009, the town went nuts. Here is one of many cartoons I drew about grabbing that historic sixth ring.
Published 02/04/09.

3 THE TOP TEN REASONS I DIDN'T GO INTO MEDICINE

ONE CHILD LEFT BEHIND

Thanks to my dad's chosen profession I am often asked, "Why didn't you go into medicine like your father?" My gut instinct is to say, "because, he's not the boss of me!" But the real reason is … I just wasn't meant to. I like to say I had an epiphany in 5th grade. This particular epiphany happened to correspond with flunking math and science. I knew then and there I was meant for other things.

I've had more than my share of odd jobs. During college and graduate school I worked as a window washer on high-rise buildings (that's kind of like a lung washer), a school bus driver, a door-to-door salesman, a self-serve gas station attendant, a caricature artist at an amusement park and a restaurant folk singer. In high school, when my dad still thought there might be a chance I wouldn't flunk science, he found me work at the hospital. One summer I wheeled patients to and from x-ray and physical therapy. Another summer I worked in the hematology lab. The guy who coined the expression "exciting as watching paint dry" obviously never watched tubes spin in a centrifuge all day. My dad even woke me up early a couple of mornings to follow him on ICU rounds. Getting up early. That was another epiphany.

After many years of struggling to put into words the reasons I chose not to go into medicine, I decided it would be easier with visual aids.

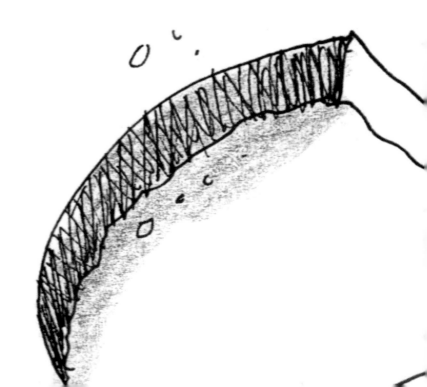

*Here are the top ten reasons
I didn't go into medicine.*

NUMBER TEN:

Dad's feet are too darn big. (Following in his
footsteps would have been almost as humiliating
as my teen years.)

NUMBER NINE:

My penmanship is too good.

NUMBER EIGHT:

There are too many big words.

NUMBER SEVEN:

"On Call" is not a concept that I embrace.

NUMBER SIX:

There is too much to remember.

NUMBER FIVE:

Malpractice insurance premiums are too high.

NUMBER FOUR:

I don't like the fashion.

NUMBER THREE:

Everyone's so darn serious.

NUMBER TWO:

I hate golf.

And the **NUMBER ONE** reason I didn't go into medicine:

THERE ARE TOO MANY BODILY FLUIDS!

4 WHERE DO YOU GET YOUR IDEAS?

NO, THEY DON'T SELL THEM ON EBAY

The question I am most frequently asked (besides "boxers or briefs?") is "where do you get your ideas?" People ask me this so matter-of-factly, as if they are asking me where I buy my shoes. Sometimes I tell them "The Stork" brings them. I would, hereby, like to debunk a few of the myths concerning where ideas really come from.

Not even the Swedes have invented an "Idea Store."

ABOVE LEFT: There are no elves that come in the middle of the night to leave behind good ideas.

ABOVE RIGHT: Ideas don't just fall from the sky, as some would have you believe.

BELOW: There is no "idea switch" to flip, although caffeine helps.

ABOVE: Capturing a good idea takes the patience of a hunter waiting to trap his prey.

BELOW LEFT: Once the germ of an idea is rolling around in my head, it feels a bit like being pregnant.

BELOW RIGHT: There is nothing prouder than a cartoonist with a newborn idea.

THE CREATIVE PROCESS

Trying to explain the creative process is like trying to explain the appeal of Carrot Top.
It defies words. But if, under extreme torture, I am forced to talk about my creative process,
I sum it up with two words: Venti Latte. Nothing inspires me like a good dose of caffeine.
As the caffeine starts to kick in, I read several newspapers, browse the internet and make a
list of potential topics. I stare at the list until one of the topics jumps off the page and says,
"pick me, you fool!" Next, I begin thinking of metaphors and/or situations that would best
illustrate what I want to say. I open my sketchbook and work up a few rough ideas. Usually,
by the time I am sketching the rough, it has already been edited in my mind for taste and
content (except for the time when I thought drawing George W. Bush milking an old woman
labeled "Social Security" was a good idea). I look over the roughs and choose the best one to
work up as a finished cartoon. Once the cartoon is finished it still has to pass muster with
the editor. As you might imagine, editors and cartoonists are from very different planets.

To most editors, punctuation
is everything.

ABOVE LEFT: I start by reading the paper and finding a good topic like a story about scientists cloning a sheep.

ABOVE RIGHT: I think, "Gee, what's so bad about a bunch of cloned sheep?"

BELOW: Well, I know what would scare ME about cloning!

ABOVE: Since most readers don't know my editor I have to translate it into a more universal fear. For instance, when Bill Clinton was in the White House, what would have frightened him the most? Cloned Newts, no doubt. *Published 02/25/97.*

BELOW: Some say the debate over whether to clone or not is already a moot point. *Published 08/21/01.*

5 CARTOONISTS ARE FROM MARS AND EDITORS ARE FROM VENUS

CAN'T WE ALL JUST GET ALONG?

There has been much written about the great adversarial relationships throughout history: Christians vs. Lions, Cowboys vs. Indians, Hatfields vs. McCoys, Star Wars Geeks vs. Trekkies … the list goes on. But not enough has been written about one of the most explosive relationships of all time: Cartoonists vs. Editors.

Ok, perhaps explosive is an overstatement, but there is definitely a disconnect. Editors have been trained their whole lives to be word doctors. They can cure a bad case of split infinitives, surgically remove a dangling modifier and make sure a colon is functioning properly. But they have no idea what to do with cartoons. They stare at them, puzzling as if they are trying to decipher ancient hieroglyphics. They won't laugh, or even smile, but they will, with a straight face, suggest using a hyphen in "zipper-challenged president." All editors (except, of course, for the brilliant editors who pay my salary) are funny-bone challenged. If, in addition to being funny, the cartoon also addresses a controversial topic, forget about it. All the editor can see are the angry faces of readers calling up to cancel their subscriptions, the newspaper equivalent of a malpractice suit.

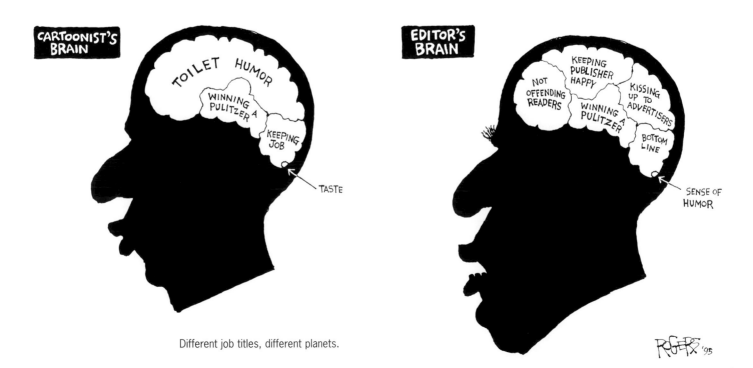

FURTHER EVIDENCE THAT CARTOONISTS ARE FROM MARS *and* EDITORS ARE FROM VENUS...

Different job titles, different planets.

PART II

Inking Butt
and Taking Names

6

WHERE'S
THE BEEF?

WHERE'S THE BEEF?

FEAR AND DRAWING ON THE CAMPAIGN TRAIL

There is no better time to be a political cartoonist than during a presidential campaign. Not because there is anything newsworthy going on. There usually isn't. The candidates will do and say anything to appear "electable." They rarely wander from their scripts, which, to be honest, sound a lot like the other candidates' scripts. It's only after one of them gets into office that they let their true colors show, leaving voters crushed and bewildered by the onslaught of broken campaign promises.

It's not the content of their campaigns, it's the saturation. During a presidential campaign the candidates do so many whistle stops, photo-ops and press conferences that they're bound to say and do more stupid things than they otherwise would. It's the law of averages. And the media is right there to cover every imperfection. Why would an otherwise sane individual agree to such intense scrutiny?

Once, in my college figure drawing class, the regular model failed to show up. Normally, the instructor would choose someone in the class to pose fully clothed. On this particular day, however, one of the female students stood up and said, "I'll model." She then proceeded to disrobe in front of us. I think my mouth remained ajar during the entire session. This didn't make sense to me. She was, after all, one of "us."

Choosing a running mate says a lot about a candidate.
Published 08/13/00.

I spent the remainder of the semester wondering whether my fellow student was a self-assured modern woman free from the puritanical hang-ups that burden the rest of us ... or just a nutjob compelled to expose herself like a flasher outside a bus station. I would ask the same question about anyone crazy enough to run for president.

BUSH-QUAYLE

BUSH-CHENEY

I'M WITH STUPID

I'M WITH STUPID

©2000 PITTSBURGH POST-GAZETTE   ROGERS

1984

My rookie year as a full-time political cartoonist was the same year the democrats made campaign history. No, I'm not talking about how they co-opted a popular phrase from a Wendy's commercial ("where's the beef") for their campaign slogan. I'm talking about how they were the first major party ticket in American history with only ONE boring white guy on it.

ABOVE: Walter "Fritz" Mondale, the Democratic presidential nominee, chose Geraldine Ferraro as his running mate. *Published 07/20/84.*

BELOW: It was a shining moment for women's rights but the fairy tale was short-lived. Whether it's 1984 or 2004, the American voters always prefer TWO boring white guys. *Published 11/07/84.*

1988

Do you remember where you were when you heard the news that George H. W. Bush had picked Dan Quayle as his running mate? Of course you do. Who doesn't? But if you still don't believe campaigns bring out the stupid in politicians, I have six words for you: Michael Dukakis in an army tank.

ABOVE: Still not convinced? Two more words: Gary Hart. Talk about stupid. Hart challenged the media to follow him. They uncovered the whole Donna Rice 'Monkey Business' and he still had the gall to enter the race! *Published 12/16/87.*

BELOW: The Democrats started out with the usual difficulties making up their mind, puzzling between Jesse Jackson, Paul Simon and Michael Dukakis. *Published 03/17/88.*

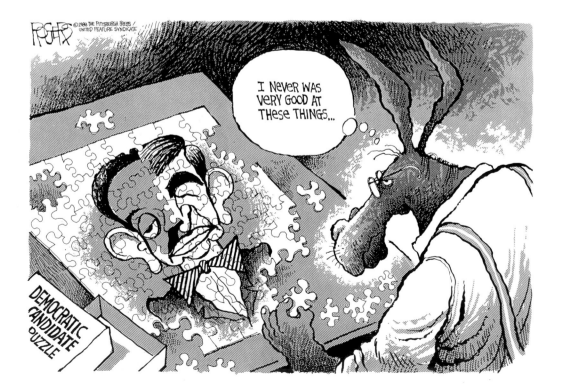

ABOVE: My choice for the Democratic nominee was based on issues I really cared about: big ears, big lips, funny looking glasses and goofy bow ties. *Published 04/10/88.*

MIDDLE LEFT: But, in the end, there was only room for one Paul Simon in the public arena. *Published 03/04/88.*

MIDDLE RIGHT: The early primaries didn't help narrow the field. *Published 03/02/88.*

BELOW RIGHT: The Democrats finally picked Dukakis as their candidate. *Published 09/20/88.*

ABOVE LEFT AND RIGHT: Meanwhile, Bush picked a young Dan Quayle for his running mate hoping he would appeal to women voters. They forgot to check his military record...and his spelling. *Published 08/10/88* and *08/12/88.*

MIDDLE: Bush had his own stupid moment when he forgot the date Pearl Harbor was bombed. Naturally, with nothing else to report, the media ate it up. *Published 09/22/88.*

BELOW: The endless droning of canned phrases made the candidates look like zombies. *Published 10/21/88.*

ABOVE LEFT: The campaign took a nasty turn as Republicans used Willie Horton to portray Dukakis as soft on crime. Dukakis fought back with all he had. *Published 10/30/88.*

ABOVE RIGHT: The voters ended up seeing a lot of mud but very little substance. *Published 10/27/88.*

BELOW: In the end, the Massachusetts Governor lost big. *Published 09/02/88.*

ABOVE: Winning the election made George H. W. Bush very happy. *Published 11/10/88.*

BELOW: It was an ugly campaign. I wonder what the next one will be like? Don't ask. *Published 11/09/88.*

1992

In 1992 incumbent George H. W. Bush vastly underestimated his opponent. I am speaking, of course, about the
economy. It went south quicker than his record-high poll
numbers. Add one charismatic Arkansas Governor and
one folksy Texas Billionaire and America had itself a
horse race!

ABOVE LEFT: The young, hip, Bill Clinton was quite a contrast to Bush.
The Republicans tried to paint Clinton as a Liberal but they ended up
looking desperate. *Published 09/04/92.*

ABOVE RIGHT: Bush refused to debate his new challenger unless it was
on his own terms. *Published 09/29/92.*

MIDDLE LEFT: Despite the fact that he was richer than 98% of American
voters, Ross Perot stuck a chord with his straight talk. He managed to
rekindle interest in a third party while garnering 20% of the popular vote.
Published 04/15/92.

MIDDLE RIGHT: Bush longed for his post-Gulf War popularity.
Published 03/29/92 .

BELOW: Not even a Texas convention could save him.
Published 08/21/92.

1996

Oh, the irony. An incumbent Democrat with what would appear to be a permanent erection vs. the Republican challenger who would go on to endorse erectile dysfunction medication. You can't make this stuff up. Bill Clinton seemed to be sleeping with every woman he met, while Bob Dole just seemed to be sleeping. In the end the voters preferred a man of action, so to speak.

ABOVE LEFT: The Republican fervor to unseat Clinton was so great it attracted all kinds of characters to join the 1996 race. *Published 02/22/96.*

ABOVE RIGHT: At one point in the campaign, the far-right-leaning Pat Buchanan actually posed in front of Mount Rushmore saying he hoped to see his own face up there some day. No, he wasn't drunk. *Published 02/25/96.*

BELOW RIGHT: In an equally confounding photo-op moment, California's anti-immigration-law-sponsoring Governor, Pete Wilson, launched his campaign from the foot of the Statue of Liberty. No, he wasn't drunk. *Published 08/31/95.*

LEFT: Meanwhile, Dan Quayle took a break from his spelling flashcards to launch his own bid for the presidency. Yes, I think he WAS drunk. He later sobered up and dropped out of the race. *Published 02/12/95.*

ABOVE: Bob Dole emerged as the GOP front-runner, much to the dismay of Republicans who were hoping for a candidate with a pulse. *Published 02/04/96.*

BELOW: Guess who's back? That's right, Ross Perot returned for another round of third party politics. He hit the campaign trail around the same time the popular movie *Clueless* hit the theaters. *Published 09/29/95.*

ABOVE LEFT: This time the two-party monopoly wasn't amused. They managed to bar him from the televised Presidential debates. Not to be outdone, the Texas billionaire paid for his own campaign infomercials. *Published 09/29/96.*

ABOVE RIGHT: Dole tried to make Clinton's character an issue in the campaign. Voters had other character issues on their minds. *Published 10/20/96.*

BELOW LEFT: Surprise, surprise. Things turned nasty as allegations of questionable campaign fundraising surfaced. *Published 10/17/96.*

BELOW RIGHT: Bob Dole reminded voters he was part of an older generation when he mentioned the "Brooklyn" Dodgers. Meanwhile, during the 1996 AL Championship Series opener at Yankee Stadium, a twelve-year-old boy leaned over the right-field wall and robbed the Orioles right fielder of the fly ball. Dole must have felt the fielder's pain. *Published 10/13/96.*

2000

Al Gore had it all sewn up. No way he could lose. Then came Florida, otherwise known as Election Purgatory. Finally, after two months of butterfly ballots, hanging chads, eye-straining recounts, Kathryn Harris' frightening make-up and the Supreme Court's frightening meddling, George W. Bush emerged as a serious proponent for the Electoral College. They're still counting votes in Broward County.

ABOVE LEFT: The voters were wired differently in 2000. *Published 01/20/00.*

ABOVE RIGHT: Al Gore, the Democratic heir apparent to Bill Clinton, lacked the limber charisma of his former running mate. His handlers decided he needed a serious makeover. *Published 07/11/00.*

BELOW: It didn' help that he claimed he created the World Wide Web. *Published 03/25/99.*

ABOVE LEFT: Old familiar faces appeared in the GOP presidential race. *Published 03/07/99.*

ABOVE RIGHT: The Republicans were busy raising record amounts of money for George W. Bush. Not even the Forbes fortune could compete. *Published 02/13/00.*

BELOW LEFT: The choice became very clear during the debates. *Published 10/31/00.*

BELOW RIGHT: Ralph Nader enjoyed his role as the spoiler. *Published 10/28/00.*

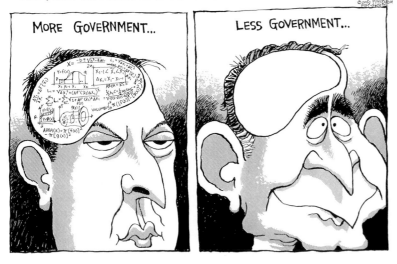

ABOVE: African American voters were turned away at the polls to help Bush's chances. *Published 12/05/00.*

BELOW: Problems with Florida's punch-hole and butterfly ballots caused confusion. *Published 11/16/00.*

ABOVE: The recount lasted two months, creating a power vacuum. *Published 11/16/00.*

BELOW: Not only did Bush have a brother who was Governor of Florida,
he had friends on the Supreme Court too. *Published 12/14/00.*

ABOVE LEFT: Gore and his lawyers made a valiant last stand. *Published 12/07/00.*

ABOVE RIGHT: But in the end, the number of votes didn't really matter. *Published 12/17/00.*

BELOW: And Bush reigned supreme. *Published 01/20/01.*

2004

John Kerry had it sewn up. No way he could lose. Sound familiar? Then came the Red State Christians with their so-called moral values. They voted for a man who would keep their children safe from gays by sending them to die in Iraq. Only in America!

ABOVE: It looked as though Howard Dean would go all the way for the Dems … until the scream heard round the world. *Published 01/25/04.*

LEFT: The soccer moms looked a little different this election. *Published 10/06/04.*

BELOW: The Democrats tried courting the new untapped voting block. *Published 08/12/03.*

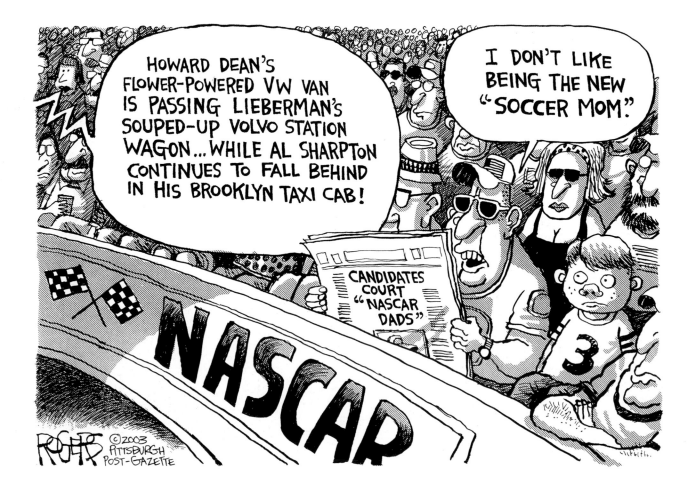

ABOVE LEFT: The "Swift Boat Veterans for Truth" attacked John Kerry's Viet Nam service. *Published 08/10/04.*

ABOVE RIGHT: The public quickly tired of talk of swift boats. *Published 08/26/04.*

BELOW: It was truly an ugly campaign. *Published 03/21/04.*

ABOVE: They accused Kerry of throwing away his medals, when in fact it was only his ribbons. *Published 05/01/04.*

BELOW LEFT: Bush downplayed the human toll in Iraq, while exploiting victims of 9/11. *Published 03/09/04.*

BELOW RIGHT: Iraq loomed large in the debates. *Published 09/28/04.*

ABOVE: Bush continued to downplay the negative. *Published 09/09/04.*

BELOW: Ralph Nader unsuccessfully tried to reprise his role as the spoiler. *Published 07/04/04.*

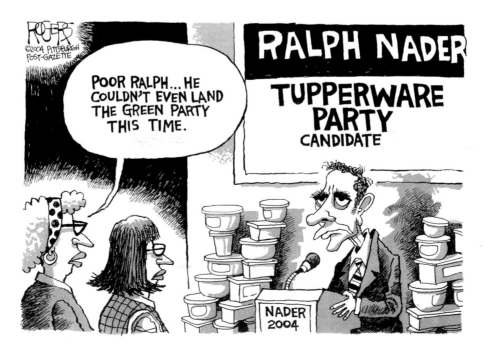

THE POLITICAL CONVENTIONS

Every four years the party faithful get together for lavish and enormous beauty pageants to crown their respective queens. Each party trots out their brightest people of color to prove their party knows what the word diversity means and what's best for the country. These monumental farces make Shakespeare look like an amateur. In terms of content, there's more news value in Janet Jackson's wardrobe malfunction. Sure, once in a while something newsworthy happens like in 1988 when Bush 41 announced that Dan Quayle would be his spelling bee partner. But for the most part, nothing really happens. That said, they are great for cartoonists. It is the one chance a cartoonist has to leave the office like a real journalist, responding directly to unfolding events. Ok, most of what's unfolding involves journalists trying to weasel their way into private parties for free booze, but at least it's being documented up close.

ABOVE: There was an exciting and inspirational new way to follow the political convention in 2000. Unfortunately, the content was the same.

ABOVE: In 2000, the GOP met in Philadelphia. The delegates were dressed flamboyantly enough to march in the local Mummers Parade.

Here are a few excerpts from a convention diary I kept during the 2004 GOP Convention in New York City.

On gaining access to the convention floor: As soon as I was out on the floor I immediately felt like an interloper. I became very self-conscious. I was afraid someone was going to spot me in the crowd and point at me, their eyes bugged out, screaming a high-pitched alien scream like the pod people in *Invasion of the Body Snatchers* after they spotted an actual human being in their midst.

On scripted conventions: Gone are the days when candidates were chosen right there on the convention floor like a WWF match. I can hear it now: "Delegates … let's rumble!" Not anymore. Now the delegates just stare glassy-eyed at the stage waiting for their instructions on when to raise their signs or clap in unison. They truly are pod people.

On Republicans getting down: If they really believe in God the way they claim to then why do they defy him? God never intended for Republicans to dance in public. It's painful to watch. They make Elaine on *Seinfeld* look like she trained with the Bolshoi Ballet. Abu Ghraib might have been more successful if they had used dancing Republicans to torture and extract information from prisoners instead of those naked photo sessions with hoods and leashes. And yet, there they were, defying their god to the music while the balloons fell like bombs on Iraq.

ABOVE: In New York City in 2004 it was hard to distinguish the right-wing delegates from the regular street crazies.

BELOW: Not wanting to talk about Bush's failed first term, the Republicans used their 2004 convention as an excuse for a full frontal attack on John Kerry.

2004 Convention Sketchbook

When I am not trying to sneak into private parties, I am working on daily sketchbook entries. Here are a few examples from the DNC in Boston and the RNC in New York City.

ABOVE: Boston, the home of John Kerry, was the site of the Democratic National Convention.

Unprecedented security marked the first political convention since 9/11 ...

Including a barrier that looked like it was constructed by Ariel Sharon ...

No one was beyond security's reach ...

ABOVE: Security was tight in Boston.

ABOVE: The 2004 Republican National Convention was held in The Big Apple. Republicans in New York City ... what an odd match. It was a bit like the Ku Klux Klan having a convention in Harlem.

Here are some excerpts from my 2008 Convention Sketch-Blog

Pittsburgh, August 22, 2008

Packing For The Convention

As everyone around me is returning from their final vacations of the summer, I am thinking about the politics of packing. I know what to pack for the beach: sunscreen, bathing suit, SpongeBob SquarePants floaties. But what does one pack for the Democratic and Republican Conventions? The DNC and RNC are back to back this election season, making for a bipartisan suitcase experience. Toothbrush: check. Shampoo: check. Barack Obama underwear: check. John McCain underwear: check. Just kidding. I don't actually have John McCain underwear.

I will try to refrain from fawning over Obama too much. I can't speak for the rest of the media.

Denver, August 26, 2008

Hillary's Big Squeeze

How in the world is Hillary going to undo the damage she did during the campaign? That's the big question everyone is asking here in Denver. You can't un-ring the bell or un-squeeze the toothpaste tube. It's out there, people! And everyone, including John McCain and his team, can use it against Obama. Hillary pulled off some pretty amazing comeback miracles during the primary season. Putting the toothpaste back in would beat them all.

Denver, August 26, 2008

Caste Credentials

I am trying my best to get a hall pass tonight to see her in action. My pass doesn't actually get me in to the hall. For those playing at home, let me explain how convention credentials work. As with all societies, political conventions have their caste system too. First, you have the Nobles: those are the high-ranking Democratic pols and rich donors. They can go anywhere they want because they have either limitless power or the money to buy it. Then you have the Clergy. They're the ones who think God gave them an all-access pass. The Clintons fall into that category. Major news anchors can fall into that category too. Then you have the Commoners which are divided into thee types. The first type of Commoner is the Burgher. Burghers are either delegates who own an estate (or who come from a state) or journalists with floor passes. The second type of Commoner is the Serf or Peasant. I am a Serf. How do I know I am a Serf? Because I have what is called a perimeter pass. We Serfs are allowed to go up to the Pepsi Center door (i.e., the drawbridge of the walled castle) but are forbidden to enter. If we try to enter they will pour scalding oil on us from the parapets. The only comforting fact about my Serfdom is that there are the even lesser Commoners. The third type is the Estateless or Homeless. "I complained about my perimeter pass until I saw a man without any pass." I think I read that in the Bible once. So, tonight

I will beg my Burgher colleague for his hall pass. I may have to give him foot massages for a month or plow his acreage but it will be worth it. For one brief moment I will no longer be a Serf. Sure, at first I will still feel sorry for my fellow serfs ... but by the end of the night I'll be the one manning the cauldron in the parapet.

Denver, August 27, 2008

Pro-Choice Party Favors

Swag is not in short supply at political conventions. There are give-aways everywhere you look with someone's logo on them. Pens, water bottles, keychains, you name it. In all my years covering conventions I have never seen a giveaway quite like the one I saw at a delegation breakfast I attended.

The pro-choice group NARAL had a table by the door and they were handing out cans that were about the size and shape of a tennis ball can. Printed on the side it said, "Yes We CAN!" The terrible pun wasn't lost on me. What was lost on me was the thought behind this market-ing idea. I thought from the look of the can that it contained springy snakes that would pop out (I've been in a few novelty stores in my time.) Instead there was a pro-choice game booklet inside, pro-choice buttons and a pro-choice beer bottle opener. I am not mak-ing this up. Inside the "fun games" booklet there were crosswords, jumbles, a connect-the-dot game and a maze where you had to find your way out of John McCain's reproductive policies.

PRO-CHOICE WHOOPIE CUSHION

Look, I am totally in favor of a woman's right to choose, but when is anything that has to do with abortion fun? And what were they thinking with that bottle opener. Do they think a pregnant woman is saying to herself, "Hmmm,

PRO-CHOICE PARTY ANIMAL

this is probably the most personal, serious and emotional decision about my body I will ever have to make ... it's Miller time!" What's next, yo-yos against the death penalty? I understand using bumper stickers and buttons to point out where you stand on an issue. But I will stick with my Homer Simpson beer bottle opener that plays a recording of Homer saying, "mmm ... beeeer!" when you use it. That seems far more appropriate than one promoting reproductive freedom.

Denver, August 28, 2008

Po' Boy Security

"The security here is off the hook!" said a delegate as he was going through the metal detector. He's right. Bus loads of SWAT teams poured into Denver and locked down the city this week. Today they are taking it up a notch. But it isn't just the Pepsi Center. I was walking through downtown yesterday (I am still looking for a protester) and I was getting hungry. I spotted a place called Bubba Gump. No, Bill Clinton hasn't opened a restaurant in Colorado. If the name sounds familiar you probably saw the movie *Forrest Gump.*

Paramount Pictures franchised the shrimp house that gets its name from the business started by Forrest and his buddy in the movie. In the movie Forrest magically shows up at all the important events in U.S. history. If I remem-ber correctly he was even at the "I have a dream" speech at the Lincoln Memorial. Since today is the anniversary of that speech, and because the food smelled really good, I decided to give it a try. Easier said than done. Before being allowed in, someone asked if they could search my bag. That's when I noticed two large security guards in uniform. They searched my bag, giving me suspicious glances while they worked. They even opened my pencil case and checked out my pens and markers. I understand the security at the Pepsi Center, but what are they afraid of at Bubba Gump? Did they think I was going to smuggle in my own shrimp or sabotage their po' boy sandwiches with rancid tartar sauce? Off the hook, indeed! Off the fish hook ...

DROP THE SHRIMP, PUNK!

Minneapolis/St. Paul, September 2, 2008

Finally, Some Protesters

If you have been reading my blog you know I have been keeping an eye out for protesters. Despite the fact that they were sighted in Denver I didn't have any luck finding them. In Minnesota my luck changed. Saturday I saw a small group of about 50 protesters. They were marching in favor of medical marijuana. They seemed very happy to be there (gee, I wonder why?) and were totally non-violent. They were yelling, "make bongs, not bombs." Sounds sensible to me! I don't know if this counts as a protest because there were only three of us watching.

Yesterday was the big sighting. According to reports, there were an estimated 10,000 protesters on the streets of St. Paul and 284 ended up getting arrested. I could see the massive protest from where I was standing, but the street was blocked and I couldn't get near them. Fortunately, I managed to run into what must have been a splinter group. It was only about 500 strong and they were marching down a street I could access.

I forged my way into the crowd and tried to speak to a marcher who had just dragged a trash can out into the street. I wanted to find out what he was protesting. Maybe he had a problem with organized trash

collection. He seemed to be part of a group dressed in fatigues and wearing bandanas. As I approached the group I could've sworn I heard a woman in the group yell, "gather round, Radical Thematicals!" She was clearly some sort of leader and raised her hand to wave in the other members. Radical Thematicals? I wasn't quite sure I heard it right. I knew "Radical" was right but I wasn't sure about the second part ... except that it ended with "aticals."

Maybe they hated the conventions of punctuation and spelling and called themselves "Radical Grammaticals." That could make for some interesting protest signs. Maybe they were anarchists who just needed a vacation and answered to "Radical Sabbaticals." I needed to find out. "What is the name of your group?" I asked. She turned and pushed me away, saying, "we don't allow press here."

Hold on. A protester who doesn't want any publicity? "The constitution gives us both a right to be here," I said to her. "You have to leave," she said more firmly. One of her cohorts, who probably weighed in at about 275 lbs., body-blocked me out of the circle they were forming. As I stumbled back trying not to fall, the woman yelled, "We're just trying to be courteous." Maybe they are the "Radical Grammaticals." She clearly has no idea what "courteous" means.

2008

Somebody pinch me, I must be dreaming. Is this the same country that elected George W. Bush twice? (or for you Lefties keeping score — is this the same country that elected George W. Bush once after watching him steal the election from Al Gore four years earlier?) When did we become so progressive? Not only did we elect Barack Obama as our first African American president, we did it after a long and exciting primary where we almost chose a woman! Forget pinching me, I like this dream.

ABOVE: It was clear from the beginning that frontrunner Hillary Clinton would have to answer for her Iraq war vote. *Published 02/13/07.*

BELOW: The historic nature of the election could not be overstated. *Published 12/23/07.*

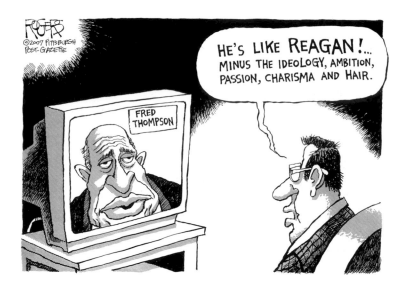

ABOVE LEFT: The Republicans were hoping Fred Thompson would be the second coming of Ronald Reagan. *Published 06/07/07.*

ABOVE RIGHT: Rudy Giuliani based his entire campaign on his mayoral leadership after 9-11. *Published 09/06/07.*

MIDDLE LEFT: Fred Thompson wasn't living up to all the hype. *Published 10/16/07.*

MIDDLE RIGHT: Hillary was evasive on many issues. *Published 10/26/07.*

BELOW: Mitt Romney was also hard to pin down. *Published 12/07/07.*

LEFT: The internet played an unprecedented role in the 2008 campaign. The CNN/YouTube debate broke new ground by having viewers pose questions to the candidates via YouTube videos. One of those videos featured an animated snowman. *Published 07/29/07.*

MIDDLE: In one debate, three Republican candidates shocked viewers by raising their hands when asked who among them did NOT believe in evolution. *Published 12/14/07.*

BELOW LEFT: "Change" became the buzzword that all the candidates fought to own. *Published 01/10/08.*

BELOW RIGHT: With the Democrats locked in a prolonged head-to-head primary battle, superdelegates became more valuable than ever. *Published 02/14/08.*

ABOVE LEFT: Families and friends were split over their allegiances to Hillary and Obama. *Published 02/26/08.*

ABOVE RIGHT: Hillary's famous 3 a.m. phone call ad tried to expose Obama's lack of executive experience. John McCain just sat back and enjoyed the fight. *Published 03/07/08.*

MIDDLE LEFT: Hillary embellished the truth a bit when she claimed she came under fire during a visit to Bosnia in 1996. *Published 03/27/08.*

MIDDLE RIGHT: Obama was criticized for calling small-town Pennsylvanians bitter people clinging to guns and religion. Meanwhile, the candidates felt the need to prove they are just like them. *Published 04/15/08.*

BELOW: Despite clear evidence to the contrary, rumors persisted that Obama was an unpatriotic Muslim who refused to wear a flag pin. *Published 07/08/08.*

ABOVE: The absurd rumors were brought to life in a controversial *New Yorker* cover. Many critics failed to see that it was satire. *Published 07/17/08.*

BELOW: John McCain called Obama a celebrity, thinking that would hurt him. It just made Obama look cooler. *Published 08/03/08.*

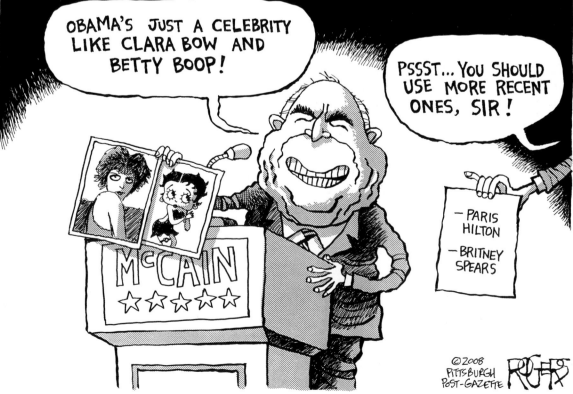

ABOVE LEFT: McCain tried to appease the GOP base by choosing Alaskan Governor Sarah Palin to be his running mate. He also tried to distance himself from the Bush administration. *Published 09/12/08.*

ABOVE RIGHT: Palin managed to energize the right wing of the party with her socially conservative views. Then again, that still didn't make her a white male. *Published 09/14/08.*

MIDDLE LEFT: She seemed a natural campaigner, distorting the truth on everything from her experience to her vote on Alaska's infamous "Bridge To Nowhere." *Published 09/16/08.*

MIDDLE RIGHT: In the midst of an economic crisis, McCain mimicked the White House by saying the economy was fundamentally strong. Oops! *Published 09/21/08.*

BELOW: Joe Biden's gaffes kept getting him into trouble. *Published 10/12/08.*

ABOVE LEFT: After Sarah Palin embarrassed herself in an interview with Katie Couric, Republicans were worried that she wouldn't be ready for the VP debate. *Published 10/02/08.*

ABOVE RIGHT: The old, affable John McCain was gone, having been replaced by some sort of Karl Rove attack dog. *Published 10/16/08.*

MIDDLE LEFT: The McCain campaign helped make a minor celebrity out of an Ohio plumber named Joe. *Published 10/17/08.*

MIDDLE RIGHT: A McCain supporter made news when she said she was attacked by Obama supporters who carved a backwards "B" on her cheek. Turns out she did it to herself and there was no attack. *Published 10/28/08.*

BELOW: When Obama won the election, I couldn't help but wonder what Lincoln would be thinking. *Published 11/06/08.*

ABOVE: It was no longer just a "White House." *Published 11/07/08.*

BELOW: Despite the historical significance of Obama's win, we still have a ways to go. *Published 11/30/08.*

7

DRAW ONE
FOR THE GIPPER

DRAW ONE FOR THE GIPPER

BEDTIME FOR RONZO

The first time I saw Ronald Reagan's hair it was love at first sight. I HAD to draw it. The rosy cheeks, wrinkled neck, squinting eyes and occasional cowboy hat were great, but it was the hair that I loved the most. He was the Grecian Formula candidate. When Halloween rolls around every year, the Reagan mask is one of the few masks where the shiny rubber hair actually looks real. Whether he was fighting communists, trading arms for hostages, piling up record deficits or ignoring the AIDS crisis, Ronald Reagan's hair looked good.

TRICKLE-DOWN REVOLUTION

The "Reagan revolution" is often described as a war against big government and taxes. To me, it looked more like class warfare, pitting the economic Red Coats (the wealthy and the military) against the economic Colonialists (the poor and middle-class.) Ron's "revolution" had a different outcome than the original. Instead of independence, we ended up shackled to record deficits. We're still waiting for something to trickle down.

Reagan believed in less government but not less military.
Published 12/07/84.

ABOVE: When it came time for budget cuts, the "best dressed" award always went to the military. *Published 02/04/86.*

BELOW: Even education took a back seat to the military. *Published 01/04/87.*

ABOVE LEFT: Reagan had trouble connecting with the poor. He claimed that the reason there were hungry people in America was because they didn't know where to go. *Published 05/23/86.*

ABOVE RIGHT: He wasn't any more compassionate to the ones providing the food. *Published 08/14/86.*

BELOW: Bruce Springsteen came out with "Born in the USA" at the same time Tip O'Neill was fighting for the American worker. *Published 09/22/85.*

WOULDN'T YOU LIKE TO BE A CONTRA TOO?

Political cartoonists live for a juicy scandal to dip their ink pens into. I used to mourn the fact that I missed the chance to draw cartoons during Nixon's Watergate era. But that was before Reagan came along and allegedly worked out a deal with Iran to hold the hostages until after the election, denying Jimmy Carter his much-needed "October surprise." That was before the hostages were traded for U.S. weapons and the proceeds were illegally diverted to support the Contras in their fight to overthrow the leftist democratically elected Sandinista government of Nicaragua. That was before the administration's cover-up and shredding of documents. That was before everyone took the fifth and, despite John Poindexter and Oliver North being found guilty, no one ever went to jail. I no longer mourn not being around to sketch Watergate. Iran-Contra made Watergate look like a shoplifting offense.

ABOVE RIGHT: Reagan tried to make the case that the Contras needed U.S. help. *Published 03/11/86.*

MIDDLE RIGHT: But the Democrats weren't buying it. *Published 03/21/86.*

BELOW RIGHT: The media started asking questions. *Published 01/02/86.*

BELOW LEFT: Reagan took the necessary precautions. *Published 01/03/86.*

ABOVE LEFT: Eventually the story of the arms-for-hostages deal broke wide open. *Published 11/12/86.*

ABOVE RIGHT: The Russians, it turned out, were supporting the other side. *Published 01/06/87.*

MIDDLE LEFT: The White House denied knowing anything about it. *Published 01/27/87.*

MIDDLE RIGHT: The president's memory was an issue even before he was diagnosed with Alzheimer's. *Published 02/25/87.*

LEFT: Ollie North didn't serve any time for his crimes. *Published 09/17/91.*

ABOVE LEFT: Instead of being charged with treason, he was treated like a hero. *Published 07/12/87.*

ABOVE RIGHT: The Gipper survived the Iran-Contra scandal. *Published 12/31/87.*

BELOW: He even survived the tell-all books that followed. *Published 05/12/88.*

SHINING MISSILE ON A HILL

Like most kids growing up in the '60s, I remember having air-raid duck and cover drills in school. In hindsight, the only thing crouching under a desk during a nuclear attack would have done is help me leave a smaller ghost shadow after being vaporized. But this was the new enemy. When Reagan dreamed of a "shining city on a hill," you can bet he planned to surround it with missile silos aimed at the Soviets. In his weekly radio broadcast on April 11th, 1984, the President, unaware that the microphone was on, joked that he had signed legislation that will outlaw Russia forever and said, "we begin bombing in five minutes."

ABOVE LEFT: Nuclear bombs are no laughing matter, especially if you're the "great communicator." *Published 08/15/84.*

BELOW: The arms race was supposed to make us feel more secure. It didn't. *Published 07/15/84.*

ABOVE LEFT: Treaties meant little to this leader of the free world. *Published 01/01/86.*

ABOVE RIGHT: He was determined to see the world his own way. *Published 03/13/86.*

BELOW: Let's not forget, he was a movie actor. *Published 12/26/84.*

INTO THE SUNSET

History has been kind to Ronald Reagan. Way too kind. I, for one, still refuse to call the D.C. airport, Reagan National. How can you name an airport after a guy responsible for firing 11,000 air traffic controllers? CBS, under pressure from conservatives, cancelled a movie about Reagan because it wasn't flattering enough. When Reagan passed away it seemed like the entire country was suffering from collective Alzheimer's.

And he certainly left his mark. *Published 12/23/88.*

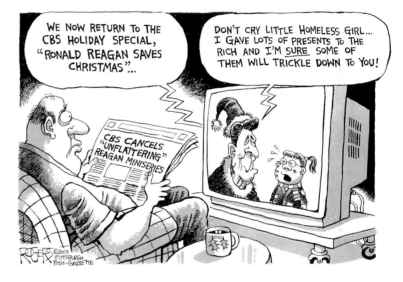

ABOVE LEFT: He left office with no regrets. *Published 01/06/89.*

ABOVE RIGHT: Now he would have time to do what he loved best: nap. *Published 08/02/85.*

MIDDLE LEFT: An airport was named after him. For some, that wasn't enough. *Published 04/29/01.*

MIDDLE RIGHT: A TV miniseries was made about him. *Published 11/06/03.*

LEFT: When Reagan passed away he was all but sainted by the media. *Published 11/12/04.*

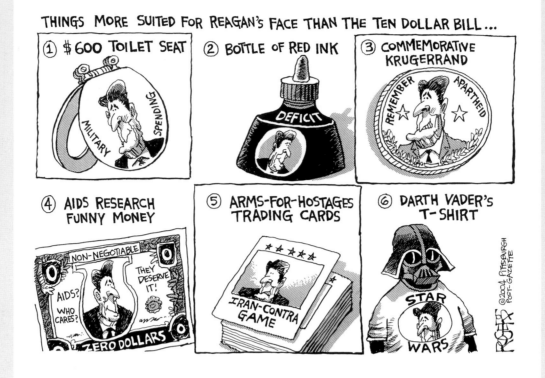

ABOVE: There was talk of putting the Gipper's face on the ten-dollar bill.
Published 06/15/04.

BELOW: The building of the Ronald Reagan Memorial was already under way.
Published 06/08/04.

8

THE SPY WHO CAME IN FROM THE COLD

THE SPY WHO CAME IN FROM THE COLD

LET'S GET NEWK-YA-LER

Growing up during the Cold War meant that once we outgrew playing "cowboys and Indians" we played "spies." I didn't mind being the Russian spy because my image of a Russian spy was the cool, debonair, Illya Kuryakin from *The Man from U.N.C.L.E.* OK. That's not totally true. My image of a Russian spy was an amalgamation of Kuryakin, Boris from *The Bullwinkle Show* and *Spy vs. Spy* from *Mad* Magazine. So, sometimes I pictured myself tall, blond and brooding. Sometimes I was short, mustachioed and spoke with a heavy accent. Other times I was a pointy-nosed bird-like character in a black hat and trench coat who carried lots of knives and explosives.

THE RUSSIANS ARE COMING

Leonid Brezhnev's eyebrows rivaled Michael Dukakis' for prime political cartoonist real estate. They were big enough to hide several medium-range ballistic missiles. He also had hair to rival Ronald Reagan's. The first time I drew him in college I knew I would enjoy targeting Russian leaders for many years to come.

The 1980s saw a resurgence in spies. *Published 12/01/85.*

ABOVE LEFT: The Cold War was all about espionage. *Published 08/26/86.*

ABOVE RIGHT: "Star Wars" technology made it hard to focus on arms cuts. *Published 11/07/86.*

BELOW LEFT: It isn't easy to pay for missiles AND put bread on the table. *Published 11/05/91.*

BELOW RIGHT: The Baltic States were ready to fly the coop. *Published 08/28/91.*

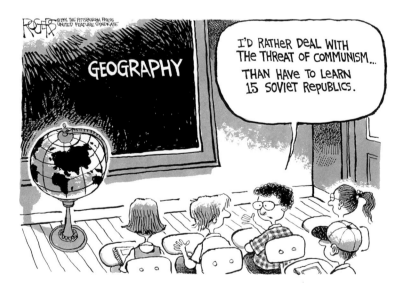

ABOVE LEFT: Despite the economy, the Russians were still in the space race. *Published 08/30/97.*

ABOVE RIGHT: Yeltsin had a hard time fighting the economic war. *Published 03/21/93.*

MIDDLE RIGHT: But he still managed to beat the communist candidate and get re-elected. *Published 06/30/96.*

BELOW LEFT: Yeltsin erratically dismissed his entire cabinet for failing to achieve economic reforms. *Published 03/26/98.*

BELOW RIGHT: The Russian economy collapsed and Yeltsin's popularity dropped almost as low as the ruble. *Published 08/27/98.*

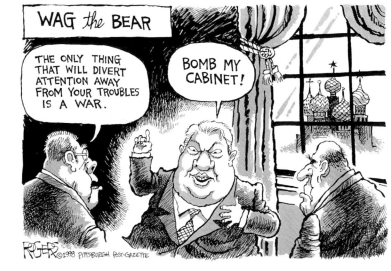

GORBY FEVER

The end of the Cold War never would have been possible without Yeltsin's predecessor, Mikhail Gorbachev. His policies of glasnost (openness) and perestroika (economic reforms) were seen by hard-liners as a betrayal of the Soviet system, but it helped create an atmosphere that encouraged serious arms talks. Plus, it must have annoyed the heck out of Ronald Reagan, who really wanted to cast Gorby to play the part of the Evil Empire.

ABOVE RIGHT: Reagan tried to paint him as trouble. *Published 01/02/85.*

BELOW: Although Gorbachev distanced himself from old Soviet ways, Afghanistan was a reminder that some iron-fisted habits die hard. *Published 01/12/87.*

ABOVE LEFT: But it was clear this was no ordinary Soviet. *Published 01/19/86.*

ABOVE RIGHT: In fact, it was sometimes hard to tell the two apart.
Published 12/11/88.

BELOW: The race to cut nukes was on! *Published 05/31/89.*

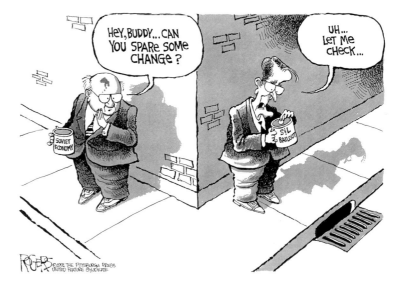

ABOVE LEFT: Gorbachev's policies were not popular at home. *Published 05/02/90.*

ABOVE RIGHT: Even though they brought him favor with the rest of the world. *Published 10/17/90.*

MIDDLE RIGHT: The Russian economy struggled to survive. *Published 06/12/91.*

BELOW LEFT: Despite all the obstacles and enemies made along the way, Gorby managed to change the face of the Soviet Empire. *Published 01/31/90.*

BELOW RIGHT: An attempted coup by hard-liners and shifting power structures made his resignation inevitable. *Published 12/10/91.*

TEAR DOWN THIS WALL

Who ended the Cold War? Sure, Reagan and Gorby both
deserve some credit but I give most of the credit to Karl Marx.
Communism was weakening the Soviet infrastructure so much
they were forced to change or die in the global economy. The
Soviets realized that full missile silos weren't as important as
full grain silos. Goodbye Lenin.

ABOVE: Especially for the old guard. *Published 02/09/90.*

RIGHT: The failures of communism were hard to admit.
Published 09/25/90.

ABOVE LEFT: The change was monumental. *Published 06/16/91.*

ABOVE RIGHT: It was the loss of an icon. *Published 11/28/89.*

MIDDLE RIGHT: Capitalism wasn't a quick-fix by any means. *Published 09/04/91.*

BELOW LEFT: The Cold War may have been over, but its economic ramifications were still being felt. *Published 12/05/89.*

BELOW RIGHT: And the wall came down. *Published 11/12/89.*

9

WE ARE
THE WORLD

WE ARE THE WORLD

DON'T MAKE ME COME OVER THERE!

I grew up watching the coverage of the Viet Nam War. It's still not over.
Published 07/15/00.

Actually, we are not the world, we only think we are. I'm not exactly sure when America's ego became so huge but my guess is it goes way back, even before we existed as a country. Trust me. Fleeing religious persecution by crossing 3000 miles of unfamiliar ocean to start a life in a land you've never even seen in a post card is not for the wilting flowers of the world. I have it on good authority that when the Mayflower landed at Plymouth Rock the Pilgrims were all wearing "We're # 1" T-shirts. If we're egotistical it's because it's in our blood.

CARPET BOMBING 2000

KFC

Pizza Hut

Nike

GAP

Coke

M

STARBUCKS

US./VIETNAM TRADE PACT

ABOVE LEFT: Communism bad, capitalism good. *Published 07/13/95.*

ABOVE RIGHT: You're either with us … or we may boycott something named after you. *Published 02/22/03.*

MIDDLE LEFT: The French are certainly not convinced of our self-proclaimed greatness. *Published 03/16/03.*

MIDDLE RIGHT: In fact, they struggle to be as non-American as possible. *Published 04/25/02.*

LEFT: We are in favor of world peace as long as it doesn't cut into our profit. *Published 08/13/91.*

ABOVE: Defense contractors, with their high-priced toilet seats, kept the money flowing. *Published 02/06/85.*

BELOW: Speaking of toilets, the military's controversial missile defense program flushed more than its share of taxpayer money. *Published 07/13/00.*

"Please pass the ice cream..."

ABOVE LEFT: Even a simple pair of pliers wasn't affordable. *Published 06/21/90.*

ABOVE RIGHT: Testosterone also plays a big part. *Published 06/02/98.*

MIDDLE LEFT: Bombing as a form of diplomacy has become more accepted in recent years. *Published 03/28/99.*

MIDDLE RIGHT: When our bombs accidentally took out a Chinese embassy in Belgrade, the military blamed it on outdated CIA maps. *Published 05/16/99.*

LEFT: Granted, waiting for the U.N. to get involved can be problematic since their record for peacekeeping is spotty. *Published 10/23/85.*

ABOVE LEFT: They often arrive in just time to pick up the pieces. *Published 07/27/95.*

ABOVE RIGHT: U.N. members aren't all known for their stellar records regarding human rights. *Published 05/02/02.*

BELOW: NATO, created to deal with the threat of nuclear war, isn't much help these days either. *Published 03/30/02.*

THE MIDDLE EAST

I have drawn a lot of cartoons about this volatile region of the world. Unfortunately, it isn't a black-and-white issue for me. I know where I stand on abortion, gun control and the death penalty but this isn't as clear-cut. The Israeli-Palestinian conflict is like any troubled relationship. Both sides are responsible for keeping the dysfunction alive. Both sides deserve blame for the violence and credit for the peace. I believe the United States' blind support of Israel only adds to the conflict.

ABOVE: In the '80s, Secretary of State George Schulz did his best to get both sides to the table. *Published 04/06/88.*

BELOW: War has been a way of life for so long nobody knows what peace looks like. *Published 11/01/91.*

ABOVE LEFT: But the world still holds out hope. *Published 07/18/91.*

ABOVE RIGHT: Both sides have trouble recognizing each other's plight. *Published 09/07/93.*

MIDDLE LEFT: One step forward, two steps back. *Published 09/26/95.*

MIDDLE RIGHT: If anyone even shows up to negotiate. *Published 04/16/02.*

LEFT: As Ariel Sharon discovered, negotiations with Arafat were always difficult. *Published 04/04/02.*

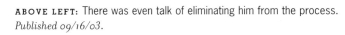

ABOVE LEFT: There was even talk of eliminating him from the process. *Published 09/16/03.*

ABOVE RIGHT: No question whose side we're on. *Published 06/30/02.*

MIDDLE LEFT: Sharon's iron fist didn't help the situation. *Published 04/18/02.*

MIDDLE RIGHT: Arafat's death was met with mixed feelings. *Published 11/14/04.*

LEFT: The quest for peace continues. *Published 09/13/03.*

BULL IN A CHINA SHOP

In 1972 Richard M. Nixon, a staunch anti-communist, normalized relations with China. Tricky Dick may not have realized that covering up Watergate and secretly taping conversations were bad ideas, but he did realize the value of diplomacy with China. Not only would it irk the Russkies in the midst of the Cold War, but the potential market for trade was gigantic. It has been a slow march to true democracy and freedom in China since then. Human rights have never been at the top of their agenda. But like a bull in a china shop, they can't be ignored.

In 1989 Communist leader Deng Xiaoping declared martial law to crack down on pro-democracy student protesters resulting in the June 4th Tiananmen Square Massacre. *Published 05/23/89.*

TOP LEFT: The courage of the Chinese students was epitomized by a famous photo of a lone protester standing down a line of tanks. President Bush (41) outraged many by sending a secret delegation to China on July 4th, 1989 to keep relations on track. *Published 07/13/89.*

TOP RIGHT: The Chinese were not known for honoring U.S. copyrights. *Published 02/07/95.*

MIDDLE LEFT: Clinton tried to get tough with trade threats. *Published 12/03/96.*

MIDDLE RIGHT: In the end human rights in China received only lip service. *Published 06/30/98.*

BOTTOM LEFT: Deng Xiaoping died in 1997. *Published 02/23/97.*

BOTTOM RIGHT: The British gave Hong Kong back to China around the same time boxer Mike Tyson made news by chewing on Evander Holyfield's ear. *Published 07/03/97.*

ABOVE: Despite human rights violations we continued to do business with China. *Published 04/10/99.*

BELOW: I wonder if Nixon knew what he was opening China up to. *Published 11/21/99.*

DESPOTS AND TROUBLE SPOTS

Before 9/11, America was kind of like a gated community just out of earshot of all the war, genocide, famine and terrorism happening in all those other neighborhoods. Occasionally we'd catch a glimpse of suffering on the 6 o'clock news. We'd shake our heads and say something must be done before flipping over to the *Seinfeld* reruns. You can't have trouble spots without a few despots. Some we hate. Some we put up with. Some we even help create and then later help overthrow.

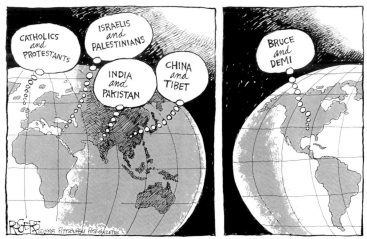

ABOVE RIGHT: The only relationships most Americans care about are the ones in *People Magazine*. *Published 07/18/98.*

MIDDLE LEFT: In the '80s Beirut became a very dangerous place. Meanwhile, the only things attacking us here at home were our pets. *Published 07/08/87.*

MIDDLE RIGHT: Muammar al-Gaddafi was accused of building chemical weapons plants in Libya. He liked to call them pharmaceutical plants. *Published 01/05/89.*

LEFT: Gaddafi and Reagan did a lot of posturing. *Published 01/27/86.*

A MINE IS A TERRIBLE THING TO WASTE...

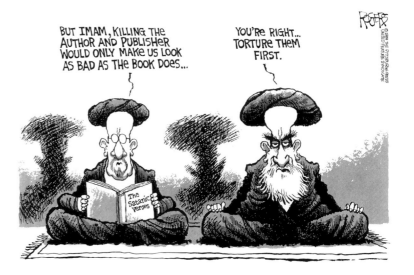

ABOVE LEFT: During the Iran/Iraq war, the Ayatollah Khomeini mined the Persian Gulf. *Published 01/10/87.*

ABOVE RIGHT: He also put a price on Salman Rushdie's head for writing *The Satanic Verses*. *Published 02/16/89.*

MIDDLE LEFT: When he died, the mourning period was brief. *Published 06/07/89.*

MIDDLE RIGHT: Iran is still considered a threat. *Published 04/20/95.*

LEFT: But the young people are not nearly as hard-line these days. *Published 06/23/98.*

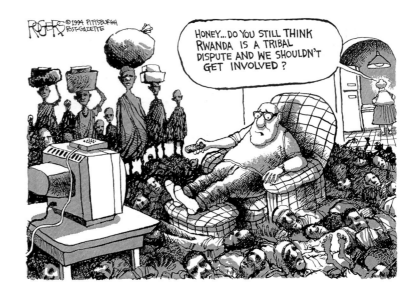

ABOVE LEFT: South Africa is still recovering from years of apartheid. *Published 06/19/91.*

ABOVE RIGHT: Images from Rwanda invaded our peaceful living rooms in 1994. *Published 07/26/94.*

MIDDLE LEFT: Belfast seems so far away and yet so close. *Published 05/26/98.*

MIDDLE RIGHT: Pol Pot, the Khmer Rouge leader responsible for the "killing fields" in Cambodia, wasn't pursued for his crimes until 1997. He fled into exile. *Published 08/20/97.*

LEFT: He passed away the following year. *Published 04/21/98.*

ABOVE LEFT: Help came quick when Kuwait's oil was threatened by Iraq. Response to Sarajevo was a different story. *Published 07/23/92.*

ABOVE RIGHT: There was much outcry when an American was caned in Singapore. It took longer to hear the outcry over genocide in Bosnia. *Published 04/09/94.*

MIDDLE LEFT: While an American president dealt with a sexual indiscretion, a Serbian president got away with murder. *Published 10/10/98.*

MIDDLE RIGHT: Boris Yeltsin continued Russia's war on Chechnya. *Published 12/11/99.*

LEFT: Ethnic hatred isn't easy to tune out. *Published 03/06/94.*

SKETCH MY LIPS

SKETCH MY LIPS

WOULDN'T BE PRUDENT NOT TO DRAW GEORGE H. W. BUSH

Like a good Vice President, George Herbert Walker Bush didn't hog the spotlight during the Reagan Administration. Everyone knows the role of the Vice-President is to help the ticket secure a certain demographic of voters during the election. In Bush's case, it was the Kennebunkport-Texan-American vote. After getting elected, he did his best to blend into the background for four years. Consequently, when Bush launched his 1988 presidential bid, I was still figuring out how to draw him. His forehead was bigger than Reagan's and his hair was thinner. He wore glasses and had slightly bushy eyebrows. His famous lips were very thin and almost non-existent, making them difficult to "draw" and nearly impossible to "read."

THE PASSING OF THE TIARA

Ronald Reagan left some big shoes to fill … or should I say a big napping couch to fill. George would have no easy time living up to the detached optimism of his predecessor, especially with real problems looming. Bush, a decorated war vet, found himself in the unenviable position of defending against public perception that he wasn't tough enough. Michael Jackson, fighting his own "wimp factor," released an inappropriately titled album. Neither he, nor Bush, made a convincing "Bad" boy.

George gets ready for his cheesecake turn.
Published 12/20/89.

ABOVE LEFT: Reagan's saccharin presidency was going to be a hard act to follow. *Published 01/17/89.*

ABOVE RIGHT: But Bush set the tone early. *Published 01/25/89.*

BELOW: Bad? I don't think so. *Published 10/14/87.*

QUAYLE UNDER GLASS

President Bush, Sr. always struck me as a fairly intelligent guy. You don't get appointed head of the CIA for being slow. That's why, to this day, it still baffles me that he chose Dan Quayle as his running mate. Don't get me wrong … whether you call it a small hiring mishap or a major political blunder, I'm thankful to the satire Gods who smiled down on editorial cartoonists that day.

ABOVE: What kind of message did it send to our kids? *Published 10/10/89.*

BELOW: What kind of message did it send to the world? *Published 05/15/91.*

ABOVE LEFT: The build-up to the Gulf War coincided with the airing of Ken Burns' *The Civil War* as seen on PBS. *Published 09/28/90.*

ABOVE RIGHT: When Bush went into the hospital for treatment of arrhythmia, the world panicked at the thought of who waited a heartbeat away. *Published 05/12/91.*

BELOW: Bush had lofty ambitions. Quayle's were more grounded. *Published 07/23/89.*

A THOUSAND POINTS OF LIGHT

The Gulf War ended up being George H. W. Bush's defining moment. Despite launching an ambitious volunteer initiative based on the phrase "a thousand points of light," it was difficult for Bush to connect with voters emotionally. While Clinton was winning with "I feel your pain," Bush came across more like "I feel your capital gains tax cut … oh, and did you see me in the Gulf War?"

ABOVE RIGHT: Bush opposed Iraq's invasion of Kuwait. *Published 01/20/91.*

MIDDLE: But looked the other way when it came to other world abuses. *Published 04/29/90.*

BELOW LEFT: He kicked booty in the Gulf. *Published 01/31/91.*

BELOW RIGHT: I was against the first Iraq war, too … but I have to give Bush (41) credit for having a plan that included an exit strategy. *Published 01/22/91.*

STUPID ECONOMY

Who could forget the democratic slogan that helped Bill Clinton win the White House away from George H. W. Bush in 1992: "It's the economy, stupid!" Bush had the highest approval rating of any former president following the Gulf War. There was no way he could lose. No way. Unless the war has been over for a while and people have a lot of time on their hands to take a serious look at their bank statements … then he could lose.

ABOVE: The popular Disney feature seemed like an appropriate metaphor. *Published 11/26/91.*

BELOW: Granted, he didn't plant the deficits, but he wasn't doing much to trim them back either. *Published 09/23/90.*

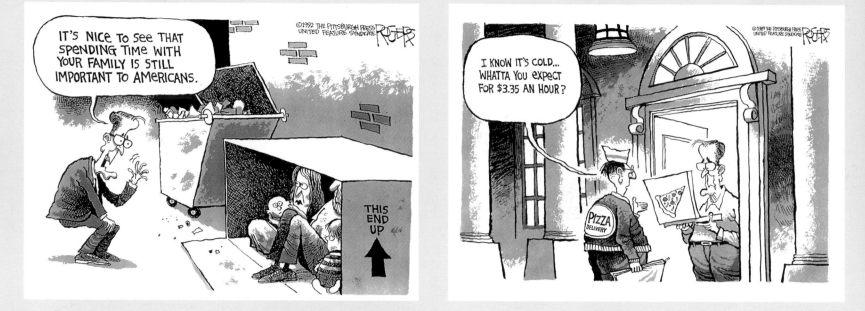

ABOVE LEFT: He talked about "family values," but gave the impression they only applied to rich families. *Published 08/27/92.*

ABOVE RIGHT: It didn't help that he vetoed a bill to increase the minimum wage. *Published 06/15/89.*

BELOW: It didn't help that his famous line "read my lips: no new taxes" became the most famous campaign promise ever broken. *Published 10/11/90.*

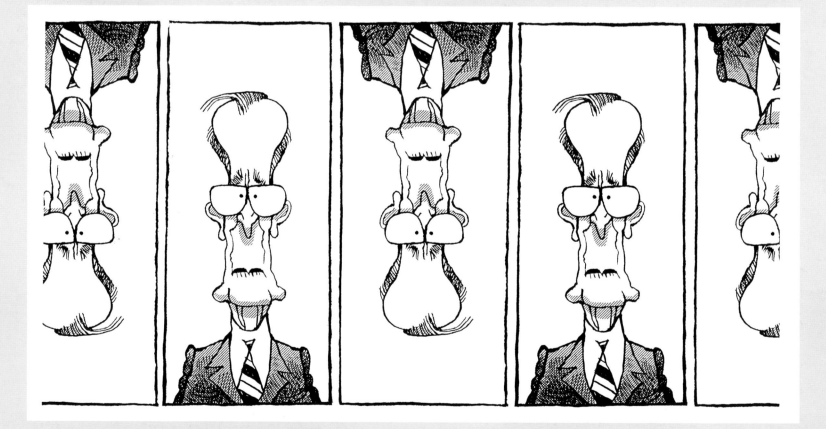

GEORGE BUSH ON TAXES

ABOVE LEFT: Hubble was having trouble and so was Bush. *Published 07/01/90.*

ABOVE RIGHT: The issue of flag burning was a convenient smoke screen. *Published 05/16/90.*

MIDDLE RIGHT: He even lost points with vegetable farmers when he declared his distaste for broccoli. *Published 05/24/92.*

BELOW LEFT: Sick with the flu, Bush vomited into the lap of Prime Minister Kiichi Miyazawa while on a state visit to Japan. After recovering he had to face other sickening thoughts. *Published 01/10/92.*

BELOW RIGHT: He talked tough … but talk wasn't worth much in this economy. *Published 01/29/92.*

ABOVE LEFT: As the election neared, the economy showed some signs of recovery … but it was already too late. *Published 10/29/92.*

ABOVE RIGHT: Bush was suddenly out of a job. *Published 11/05/92.*

BELOW: But he did get a Presidential Library. *Published 11/09/97.*

11

WHY JOHNNY
CAN'T READ GOOD

WHY JOHNNY CAN'T READ GOOD

AMERICA'S DUNCE CAP

Every year a new study comes out showing how far behind the rest of the world the American educational system is. My own experience with public education seems to support the research. I am the worst speller in the world. I'm not exagerating. My spelling is whorendous. Not to mention the large chunks of literature, history and philosophy that seem to be missing from my brain. I never read *Treasure Island* but I could write a hundred book reports about *Gilligan's Island*. So, who is to blame for my lack of education? Is it my teachers' fault for being underpaid and overworked? Is it my parents' fault for passing on the dumb genes or not banning television? Can massive amounts of Captain Crunch cause brain damage? It's hard to say, but not hard to draw cartoons about.

This cartoon was drawn in the eighties before we had 9,000 channels, many devoted to geography. *Published 08/03/99.*

NO WONDER BILLY FLUNKED GEOGRAPHY... WE DON'T GET A GEOGRAPHY CHANNEL.

CLICK CLICK

MTV

TOP: You can blame the TV or the holder of the remote. *Published 09/01/92.*

BOTTOM: Most parents went to American schools too. *Published 12/13/94.*

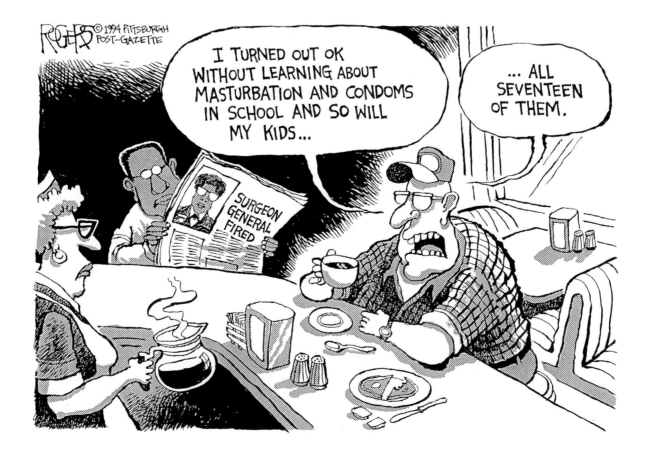

TOP: If you are looking for someone to blame, you might as well start at the top. *Published 08/15/99.*

BOTTOM: Teaching for the test doesn't seem to be working. *Published 09/16/97.*

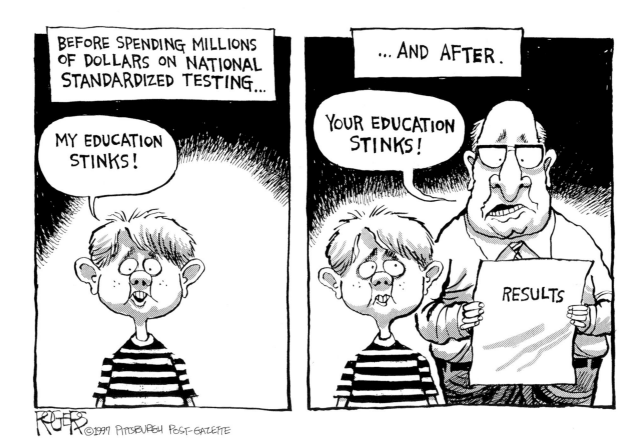

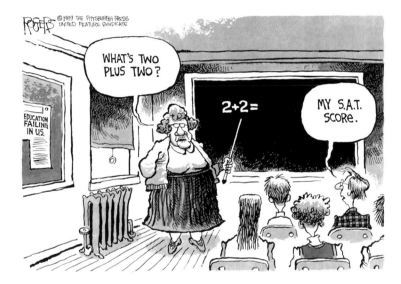

TOP LEFT: It is as simple as basic math to make fun of poor student performance. *Published 02/07/92.*

TOP RIGHT: OK, even basic math isn't simple for us. *Published 02/03/89.*

MIDDLE LEFT: But it's usually on the exam. *Published 05/04/89.*

MIDDLE RIGHT: Not even our own history is safe from neglect. *Published 05/14/02.*

BOTTOM LEFT: Sorry, no extra credit for pop culture references! *Published 07/20/89.*

BOTTOM RIGHT: Leave no president behind. *Published 09/28/89.*

TOP LEFT: After high school it doesn't get any easier. College can be expensive. *Published 05/10/85.*

TOP RIGHT: Graduates enter the dismal job market looking for ways to pay off their student loans. *Published 06/10/93.*

BOTTOM: Did I mention the dismal job market? *Published 05/07/02.*

12

IT'S THE
ECONOMY, STUPID!

IT'S THE ECONOMY, STUPID!

RAISING THE MINIMUM RAGE

My first real job, not counting mowing lawns, delivering newspapers or drawing cartoons for my dad's medical lectures, was as a busboy at a local restaurant. I was 15. I would finally be putting my freshly minted social security card to use. I opened a checking account so I would have a safe place to deposit all of my busboy riches. When my first paycheck came, I thought there had been a mistake. Half my money was missing. According to the pay stub it apparently went to someone called FICA. Who was this FICA and why had she taken a large chunk of my pay? Someone told me that FICA was another name for Uncle Sam. As far as I knew I didn't have an uncle named Sam. This was getting confusing.

Nothing motivates people like the almighty dollar.
Published 01/16/87.

ABOVE LEFT: The penny doesn't buy what it used to. *Published 05/29/03.*

ABOVE RIGHT: When the economy is faltering, consumer anxiety can set in. *Published 01/15/92.*

MIDDLE LEFT: Consumer anxiety usually means bad Christmas gifts. *Published 12/02/90.*

MIDDLE RIGHT: Hey, there's always the lottery. *Published 01/14/03.*

HANDS ACROSS WALL STREET

Ironically, the same decade that brought us charity events like "Hands Across America," "Farm Aid" and "We Are The World," also brought us insider trading. Not even the generosity of Dylan, Springsteen or Jacko could prevent the 1980s from being dubbed the "decade of excess."

ABOVE: We are the crooks. We are the burglars. *Published 05/22/86.*

BELOW: We are the ones who make a darker day, so let's start stealing. *Published 02/18/87.*

THE LATEST ECONOMIC INDICATOR

ABOVE LEFT: Fluctuations in the market can be hair-raising. *Published 01/03/87.*

ABOVE RIGHT: A tough week on Wall Street is one thing. *Published 09/16/86.*

MIDDLE LEFT: A stock market crash is another. *Published 01/16/87.*

MIDDLE RIGHT: It didn't get any easier for investors after the dot com bubble burst at the end of the '90s. *Published 09/06/98.*

BELOW RIGHT: And recent episodes of corporate greed have kept the market running scared. *Published 07/14/02.*

THE RUNNING of the BULL

GIVING US THE BUSINESS

If money is the "root of all evil," politics is one big, fat evildoer. Special interest money is running America. Although the Republicans are deeper in the pockets of big business than the Dems, greed is bipartisan. More government, less government, it doesn't matter. They still take their cut and stick the taxpayers with the bill. The rich get richer and the poor get poorer. Note to Ronald Reagan: Maybe you should have called it "trickle-UP economics."

Everybody needs a little help. Who do we turn to? *Published 07/30/91.*

SECURITY BLANKETS...

ALAN GREENSPAN IN LOVE

ABOVE LEFT: The Fed was a comfort to investors when Greenspan was at the helm. *Published 01/06/00.*

ABOVE RIGHT: Maybe it was his cautious pessimism. *Published 11/17/02.*

MIDDLE LEFT: Not even Greenspan could put a damper on Bush's stubborn optimism. *Published 08/17/02.*

MIDDLE RIGHT: The kids are the real winners. *Published 10/19/03.*

LEFT: Remember…this is the government that brought you the IRS. *Published 04/09/91.*

ABOVE: IRS agents used to be known for using harsh tactics. *Published 09/25/97.*

BELOW: Today, they claim to be a kinder, gentler IRS. *Published 10/23/97.*

ABOVE: Putting your money in a Savings and Loan is safe, right? *Published 12/30/88.*

BELOW: Run for your life! *Published 06/13/91.*

ABOVE LEFT: Of course, a job would help. *Published 02/07/93.*

ABOVE RIGHT: A job in this country, that is. *Published 01/27/04.*

MIDDLE LEFT: Save the American worker. *Published 06/20/86.*

MIDDLE RIGHT: And while you're at it, the middle class is also an endangered species. *Published 02/23/92.*

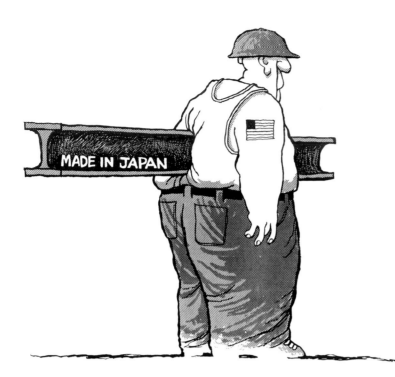

STEELHENGE

ABOVE LEFT: Nothing says "loss of American jobs" like the steel industry. *Published 09/10/84.*

ABOVE RIGHT: Steelworkers are the lost civilization. *Published 08/03/86.*

BELOW: You can't mention Pittsburgh and steel without referencing the movie Flashdance. *Published 12/06/03.*

ABOVE: The phrase "Made in America" no longer means it's the best. *Published 12/02/97.*

BELOW: The Japanese may have lost WWII, but they're winning the trade war. *Published 03/04/90.*

ABOVE LEFT: The desire for trade can encourage odd marriages. *Published 05/28/00.*

ABOVE RIGHT: The world is a tough place, even for a deficit-free powerhouse. *Published 10/06/98.*

MIDDLE LEFT: Corporate America can't save us … they're too busy filing for bankruptcy. *Published 01/01/87.*

MIDDLE RIGHT: Even moguls like the Donald have had to diversify. *Published 01/14/88.*

LEFT: America's ego is being outsourced. *Published 02/17/04.*

ABOVE: High-tech firms are downsizing. *Published 05/08/01.*

BELOW: One field that is growing: whistle-blower. *Published 12/28/02.*

GIVE US YOUR POOR

Caring for the poor and disenfranchised used to be the mission of the Democratic party. Unfortunately, bleeding-heart liberals in government are disappearing quicker than rust-belt jobs. Even Clinton co-opted traditionally Republican ideas about welfare reform and spending cuts. These days, welfare amounts to funding the construction of new stadiums for rich sports teams.

ABOVE: They say the poor will always be with us. *Published 03/23/90.*

BELOW: Unfortunately, the bureaucracy in Washington will always be with us, too. *Published 03/26/00.*

ABOVE LEFT: Sometimes the ones helping the poor help themselves as well. *Published 03/01/92.*

ABOVE RIGHT: The kids are the real losers. *Published 07/27/96.*

MIDDLE LEFT: Ignoring the poor is a bipartisan practice. *Published 09/21/95.*

MIDDLE RIGHT: The Republicans have just had more practice. *Published 07/15/99.*

LEFT: If only harming the poor were a guillotine-able offense. *Published 03/10/02.*

ABOVE: Forget the poor ... we've got a game to go to! *Published 04/26/98.*

BAILOUT MADNESS

In recent years, Americans have seen their jobs outsourced, pensions dissolved, homes foreclosed and health-care plans taken away. Predatory lenders and sub-prime mortgages caused the bottom to drop out of the housing industry and Wall Street panicked. Washington scrambled to stem the bleeding by bailing out everyone from banks to mortgage lenders to the auto industry. By 2008, some economists were calling it the worst economy since the Great Depression. Where is FDR when you need him?

ABOVE: Outsourcing, normally aimed at blue-collar jobs, was affecting white-collar workers as well. *Published 05/12/05.*

BELOW: In the new internet age, identity theft was on the rise. *Published 03/15/05.*

ABOVE LEFT: The income gap continued to grow. *Published 06/23/06.*

ABOVE RIGHT: For some workers, retirement was no longer an option. *Published 07/16/06.*

MIDDLE LEFT: Homeowners and mortgage lenders were both feeling the pain. *Published 08/19/07.*

MIDDLE RIGHT: Toys imported from China were found to contain lead. Meanwhile, the dollar was dropping like a lead balloon. *Published 11/2/07.*

LEFT: U.S. debt was being bought up by China. *Published 01/22/08.*

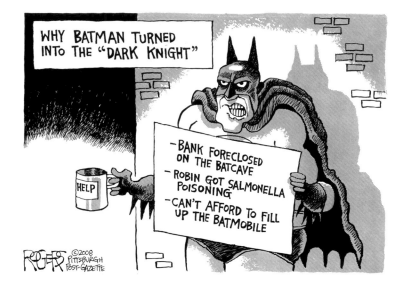

ABOVE LEFT: Our ailing economy was definitely contagious. *Published 01/27/08.*

ABOVE RIGHT: Starbucks began closing stores. When we can't afford our precious four-dollar cup of coffee, you know we're in trouble. *Published 07/06/08.*

MIDDLE LEFT: In the midst of the downturn, the latest Batman movie was released. *Published 07/20/08.*

MIDDLE RIGHT: Washington seemed more concerned about the banks than the suffering homeowners. *Published 07/27/08.*

LEFT: Even pro-deregulation Republicans were calling for regulation. *Published 09/23/08.*

ABOVE: Bush seemed uneasy in his role as cheerleader for the government bailout. *Published 09/25/08.*

BELOW: Nothing was scarier than the most recent 401(k) statement. *Published 10/03/08.*

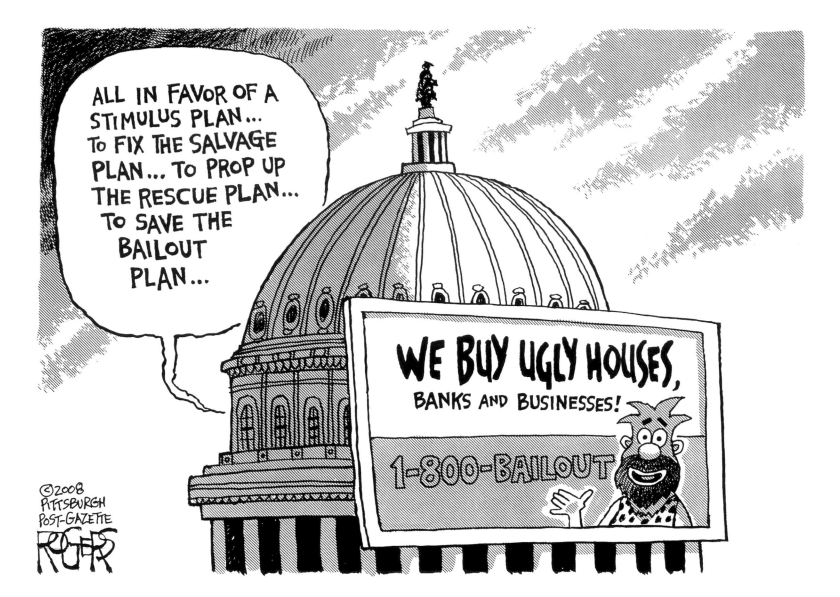

ABOVE: If the first bailout doesn't work, try, try again. *Published 11/25/08.*

BELOW LEFT: Even former Fed chairman, Alan Greenspan, regretted his deregulation gospel. *Published 10/26/08.*

BELOW RIGHT: The first time the Big Three automakers went before Congress to make their case for a bailout, they flew in their corporate jets and showed up without concrete plans. They were denied the money. Two weeks later, they returned to Washington, D.C. by car, humbled and ready. *Published 12/09/08.*

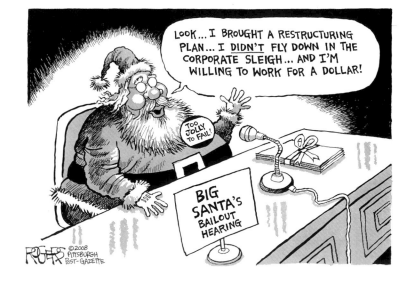

13

BUBBA'S IN
THE HOUSE

BUBBA'S IN THE HOUSE

AN AFFAIR TO REMEMBER

Combine the political savvy of FDR, the folksiness of Will Rogers, the sex appeal of JFK and the coolness of Elvis. What do you get? Bill Clinton. The Republicans knew he was the Democratic Party's messiah and immediately began a campaign to crucify him. They flogged him for eight long years but they never managed to break his spirit. Will the Democrats ever find another candidate with his charisma and appeal? Probably not. But, like the Fleetwood Mac song that was played over and over during the first Clinton campaign says, *"don't stop thinking about tomorrow."*

Bill gets sworn in.
Published 01/21/93.

DAILY AFFIRMATION

ABOVE: Clinton apologizes for trying to do too much in his first hundred days. *Published 05/08/93.*

BELOW: He was such a wonk that even vacations turned into work. *Published 08/22/93.*

ABOVE LEFT: While the country focused on whether the President wore boxers or briefs, Cinton wanted to talk about health-care reform. *Published 05/24/94.*

ABOVE RIGHT: Unfortunately for Bill, everyone had a different idea about which way to go. *Published 07/07/94.*

BELOW: Congress proved to be a sticking point. *Published 08/28/94.*

RIGHT: Eventually, the Republicans had their way. *Published 09/25/94.*

ABOVE LEFT: Whitewater also provided some troubled waters for the Clintons. *Published 01/11/94.*

ABOVE RIGHT: Much to the GOP's dismay, Dan Quayle indicated he would try to run against Clinton in '96. *Published 05/12/94.*

MIDDLE LEFT: Bimbogate began to surface around the time a live-action version of The Flintstones hit the theaters. *Published 05/01/94.*

MIDDLE RIGHT: The media ignored the important stuff. *Published 05/31/94.*

LEFT: Paula Jones wasn't the only woman Clinton needed to distance himself from. *Published 01/14/96.*

Hillary claimed she was having conversations with Eleanor Roosevelt. *Published 06/24/96.*

CONVERSATIONS WITH THE DEAD...

ABOVE LEFT: Around the same time Hillary was communing with F.D.R.'s wife, the movie Independence Day showed a scene of the White House being attacked by aliens from outer space. *Published 07/04/96.*

ABOVE RIGHT: Women dogged Clinton but men like Bob Dole were not a threat. *Published 06/27/96.*

BELOW LEFT: Clinton won a second term easily, but that didn't put an end to his problems. *Published 01/12/27.*

BELOW RIGHT: It was tough to get a clear picture of what kind of Presidency he was having. *Published 05/29/97.*

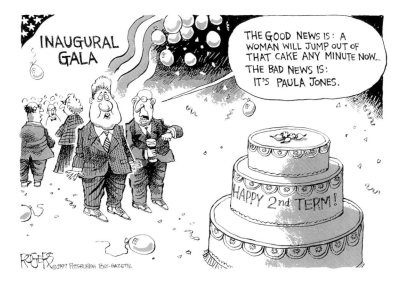

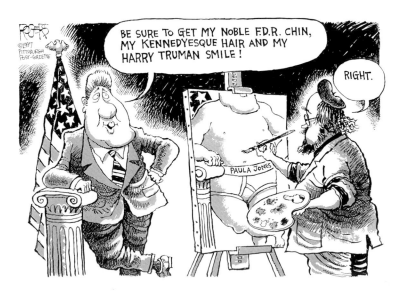

I FEEL YOUR PAIN

I once shook hands with Bill Clinton when he stopped by the newspaper to meet our editorial board during the 1992 campaign. It's true what people say about him. He grasps your hand and looks into your eyes as if he's known you his whole life. He made me feel like I was the only one in the room. When he went on TV and said, "I feel your pain," I believed him.

ABOVE RIGHT: Clinton seemed to be a magnet for unflattering news coverage. *Published 07/21/94.*

BELOW: The President visits the flood victims in middle America. *Published 07/16/94.*

ABOVE LEFT: He did his best to hold it together. *Published 07/28/96.*

ABOVE RIGHT: Accusations of campaign finance impropriety surfaced. *Published 01/30/97.*

MIDDLE LEFT: The timing was not good. *Published 09/10/98.*

BELOW LEFT: Congress ignored funding for more important needs. *Published 08/16/98.*

BELOW RIGHT: Even Whitewater wouldn't die as long as long as the GOP had their way. *Published 09/24/00.*

ET TU, MONICA

Hillary called it a vast right-wing conspiracy. She was right. The Clinton-haters poured time and money into finding anything to bring down Bill Clinton. It was a witch-hunt the likes of which we hadn't seen since the McCarthy era. If they had asked me, "Are you now or have you ever been interested in wasting $400 million of taxpayer money to investigate whether the President fooled around on his wife?" I would have said, "No, but I'd be happy to name names of those who are."

ABOVE LEFT: The Monica Lewinsky scandal unfolded like a Greek tragedy. *Published 03/17/98.*

BELOW: Clinton is caught lying about the affair when he tries to finesse the definition of the word "is." *Published 09/22/98.*

DISASTROUS STORMS EXPLAINED...

ABOVE LEFT: Clinton tried his best to keep the focus off his indiscretions. *Published 01/27/98.*

ABOVE RIGHT: The unfolding scandal was both repulsive and compelling. *Published 01/29/98.*

MIDDLE LEFT: The ubiquitous coverage overshadowed everything else, including the weather. *Published 03/12/98.*

BELOW LEFT: Even baseball's exciting race for the home run record was no match. *Published 08/25/98.*

BELOW RIGHT: Linda Tripp tried to act like she did what any self-respecting friend would have done. *Published 10/11/98.*

ABOVE LEFT: The real star of the show was the infamous "blue dress." *Published 08/04/98.*

ABOVE RIGHT: Ken Starr launched an investigation that seemed way too personal. *Published 03/07/98.*

BELOW LEFT: No one was beyond his reach. *Published 01/31/98.*

BELOW RIGHT: The Starr Report ended up reading like an extended version of Penthouse Forum. *Published 09/12/98.*

ABOVE LEFT: Clinton's sins seemed so tame compared to the sins of presidents past (and future). *Published 09/27/98.*

ABOVE RIGHT: He tried to conduct state business as usual. *Published 09/03/98.*

BELOW LEFT: He even tried to secure his legacy. *Published 07/09/00.*

BELOW RIGHT: Most Americans didn't approve of Clinton's personal conduct but they approved of what he was doing for the country. *Published 01/25/98.*

ABOVE: Some even saw Bill Clinton as a hero. *Published 11/01/98.*

BELOW: In the end, partisanship won out and he was impeached.
Published 12/24/98.

14

ANGRY
WHITE MALES

ANGRY WHITE MALES

WE'RE TIRED OF BEING OPPRESSED

One Democratic Party's nightmare is a political cartoonist's dream. Newt Gingrich, the Speaker of the House who orchestrated the 1994 Republican Revolution and created the notorious "Contract With America," has been described as a visionary and a bomb-thrower. It was the bomb-thrower I liked to draw.

Oddly enough, Newt was incredibly similar to his nemesis Bill Clinton. Both grew up in the South, avoided the draft, smoked pot and allegedly committed adultery. In fact, Mr. Family Values even asked his first wife for a divorce while she was recovering from cancer surgery. Nice bedside manner, Dr. Gingrich!

The 1994 mid-term elections were good for the Republicans. *Published 11/10/94.*

ABOVE: The GOP credited angry white males for their victory in 1994.
Published 11/15/94.

BELOW: Newt was quick to demonize the Dems. *Published 11/05/94.*

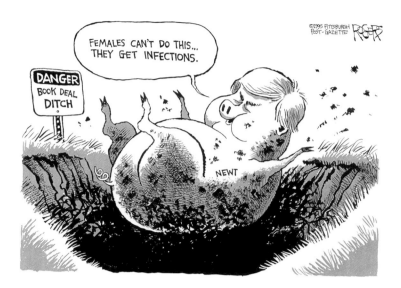

ABOVE LEFT: Newt said women were not suited for combat (living in a ditch) because "they get infections'' while men were "little piglets." His lucrative book deal proved half his theory. *Published 01/22/95.*

ABOVE RIGHT: He did his best to eliminate federal arts funding. *Published 03/19/95.*

RIGHT: He even wanted to cut school lunches. *Published 03/05/95.*

BELOW: And eliminate the programs of FDR. *Published 04/16/95.*

ABOVE LEFT: Forrest Gump he wasn't. *Published 02/19/95.*

ABOVE RIGHT: At first Newt appeared to be the best weapon of the "Republican Revolution." *Published 01/26/95.*

MIDDLE LEFT: But it soon became clear that he was just a bomb waiting to go off. *Published 12/06/94.*

MIDDLE RIGHT: He once whined about his seat assignment on Air Force One. *Published 11/18/95.*

LEFT: His fights with Clinton were trash TV material. *Published 05/03/98.*

GOP FAMILY VALUES

Newt isn't the only Republican to claim a "monopoly" on
"family values" while indulging in questionable behavior.
The list is too long to mention in full. Granted, the Democrats
have had their share of sins, but they usually aren't passing
themselves off as moral missionaries like the "family values"
Republicans.

RIGHT: The defenders of traditional marriage liked the tradition
so much they tried it more than once. *Published 09/26/96.*

BELOW: Bob Packwood resigned after charges of sexual misconduct.
Published 08/29/95.

ABOVE: William Bennett spent the royalties from his best-selling Book of Virtues on his gambling habit. *Published 05/08/03.*

BELOW LEFT: It wasn't the most mature period of American politics. *Published 01/07/97.*

BELOW RIGHT: The GOP insisted their preoccupation with Clinton wasn't a "Witch Hunt." *Published 07/13/97.*

THE OLDEST LIVING CONFEDERATE SENATOR TELLS ALL...

THE GOP's NEW DEFINITION OF "CHECKS AND BALANCES"...

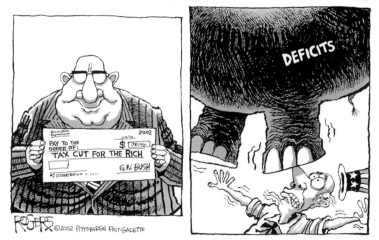

NEWS ITEM: BOB DOLE ENDORSES IMPOTENCY DRUG

ABOVE LEFT: Strom Thurmond continued to stick to the old ways of thinking. *Published 12/09/95.*

ABOVE RIGHT: Through it all, they never stopped fighting for their constituents. *Published 11/09/02.*

MIDDLE RIGHT: Bob Dole eventually gave up the fight and focused on other pressing issues. *Published 01/09/99.*

BELOW: God bless 'em, everyone. *Published 11/26/94.*

CAPITOL SALE

While conservatives are more likely to end up in one of my cartoons, corruption and stupidity tend to be bipartisan traits. Elected officials who claim to vote their conscience aren't necessarily lying. The problem is, their consciences can be bought. In fact, Congress' motto was "show me the money" long before Cuba Gooding, Jr. shouted these words at Tom Cruise in *Jerry Maguire*. Capitol Hill is the only place in America where flag burning is considered a terrorist attack and corporate sponsorship equals patriotism.

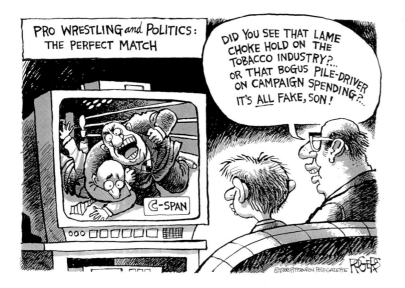

ABOVE RIGHT: Does anyone else find it funny that we entrust our money to those least likely to use it wisely? *Published 03/18/92.*

MIDDLE LEFT: They pretend to be wrestling with the moral issues, but we know better. *Published 11/08/98.*

MIDDLE RIGHT: Once in a while, elected officials try to wean themselves away from lobbyists. *Published 05/15/94.*

BELOW LEFT: They may even try some kind of campaign finance reform. *Published 02/28/02.*

THE DEBATE OVER CAMPAIGN FINANCE REFORM CONTINUES...

ABOVE: In the end, we know who they really represent. *Published 03/20/01.*

BELOW LEFT: The NRA shoots from the wallet. *Published 06/20/90.*

BELOW RIGHT: Big tobacco's wallet is equally dangerous. *Published 07/11/98.*

ABOVE LEFT: Is Congress worried that flag burning will become a national holiday? *Published 06/23/89.*

ABOVE RIGHT: The only thing more anti-American than flag burning is federal funding for the arts. *Published 07/18/89.*

BELOW: In fact, Congress once saw fit to edit out any negative images from a federally funded exhibit about the atomic bomb-dropping Enola Gay. *Published 01/31/95.*

KING OF THE ANGRY WHITE MALES

When it comes to scandal in Washington, nothing compares to Watergate. And when it comes to angry white men, nobody compares to Tricky Dick. I was too young to cover him while he was in office, but who could resist drawing that ski-nose and five o'clock shadow every now and then?

ABOVE: The scandal to beat all scandals. *Published 06/23/02.*

MIDDLE LEFT: The U.S. Postal Service even issued a Nixon stamp. *Published 11/22/94.*

MIDDLE RIGHT: Now they'll have to give stamps to all the angry white males. *Published 05/21/95.*

LEFT: Historians were kind to Nixon. *Published 05/22/94.*

BELOW: It came out that he may have taken mood-altering drugs. Thank goodness for modern medicine. *Published 08/31/00.*

15

WOMEN ON
THE VERGE

WOMEN ON THE VERGE

THE MYTH OF EQUAL RIGHTS

Some of my best friends are women. Really. I'm sure you could say the same. But let's face it. We still treat women like second-class citizens. We call them equals but we pay them a lot less. American women have had the right to vote for almost a century but, aside from the occasional star-struck intern, we have yet to see one in the Oval Office, although Hillary came close to changing that in 2008. I doubt that a handful of cartoons will make much of a dent in the fight for equality … but I'll keep trying.

OK, so we're not the worst in the world. We could still do better.
Published 09/02/95.

ABOVE LEFT: Changing the rules at a few old boys clubs isn't enough. *Published 06/24/88.*

ABOVE RIGHT: Speaking of old boys clubs ... *Published 04/17/94.*

BELOW LEFT: Barefoot and pregnant is the Church's preference. *Published 09/11/94.*

BELOW RIGHT: What does God really think about the treatment of women? *Published 10/15/91.*

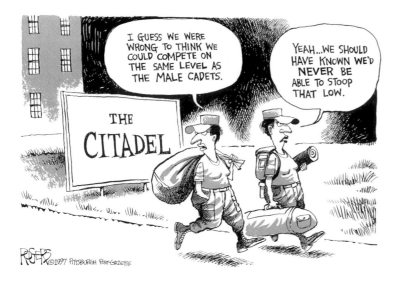

ABOVE LEFT: If you still need more abuse, join the military. *Published 01/14/97.*

ABOVE RIGHT: We have met the enemy … they're men. *Published 04/08/93.*

BELOW: It gives new meaning to the term "combat." *Published 05/01/93.*

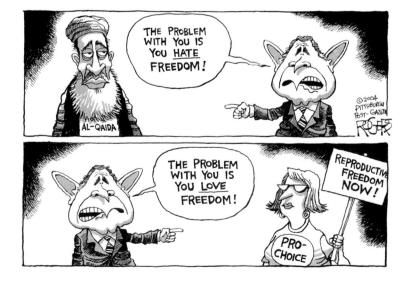

ABOVE LEFT: If the military isn't for you, any workplace will do. *Published 05/02/93.*

ABOVE RIGHT: Granted, biologically men and women are different. *Published 07/18/02.*

MIDDLE LEFT: Women are more prone to invasive politics. *Published 05/26/91.*

MIDDLE RIGHT: Questions of ownership are inevitable. *Published 03/29/96.*

BELOW LEFT: Reproductive decisions become acts of patriotism. *Published 04/27/04.*

ABOVE LEFT: Early programming is essential in teaching women about their roles. *Published 05/13/92.*

ABOVE RIGHT: Don't forget about body image … society has something to say about that, too. *Published 05/24/97.*

BELOW: It is a tough lesson to unlearn! *Published 11/25/97.*

16

SICK CARTOONS

SICK CARTOONS

TURN YOUR HEAD AND LAUGH

Health care has become
unaffordable for most.
Published 05/09/91.

This is not your father's health care system. It definitely isn't mine. My father started medical school in the fifties. It was a simpler time then. Doctors were respected. Kids wanted to grow up to be one. Mothers wanted their daughters to marry one. Television shows glorified them. Not anymore. Today's insurance company-driven world of medicine has turned Dr. Kildare into Dr. Kill-joy. Instead of patient care the physicians are practicing HMO care. Premiums have gone through the roof. The list of things covered is getting smaller while the insurance companies are getting bigger.

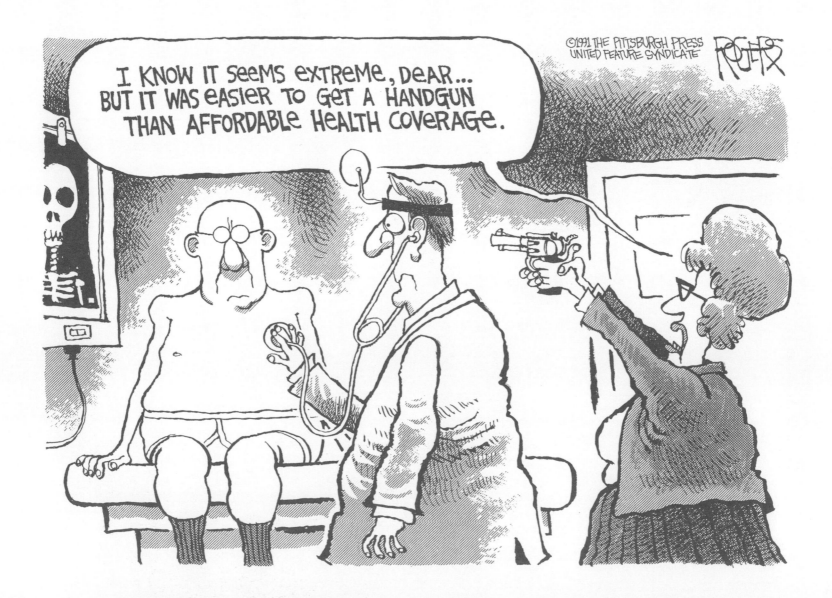

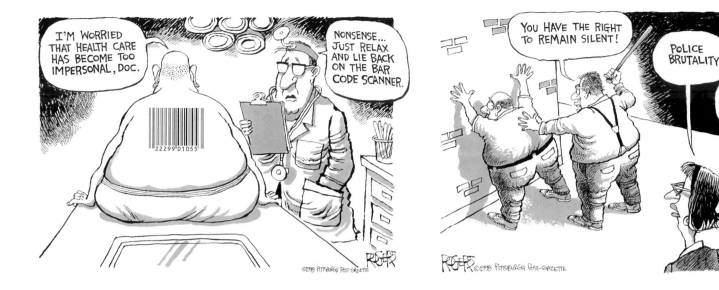

ABOVE LEFT: Managed care physicians are not known for their bedside manner. *Published 07/26/98.*

ABOVE RIGHT: In fact, dealing with your provider can be downright brutal. *Published 07/19/98.*

BELOW: My momma told me, "You better shop around." *Published 07/08/01.*

RECENT STUDIES SHOW

I love scientific studies. Not because dedicated researchers toil away in hospital laboratories finding cures for the sick of the world. Not because these studies give us insight into who we are as human beings. No, I like them because they make great fodder for cartoons. Most people can't tell you the amount of the federal deficit, but they can tell you their cholesterol level.

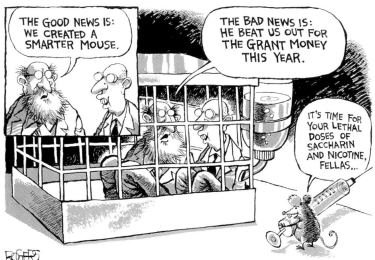

ABOVE RIGHT: Why do scientists always experiment on rats and mice? *Published 01/07/96.*

MIDDLE LEFT: It is only a matter of time before the tables are turned. *Published 09/07/99.*

MIDDLE RIGHT: The world's obsession with looking younger fuels a lot of studies. *Published 01/28/88.*

LEFT: Men and women alike are equally as vain. *Published 08/24/88.*

ABOVE: Losing weight is another obsession. *Published 12/03/94.*

BELOW LEFT: Stress has been linked to other ailments. *Published 02/18/92.*

BELOW RIGHT: News about the effects of stress is also stressful. *Published 03/09/93.*

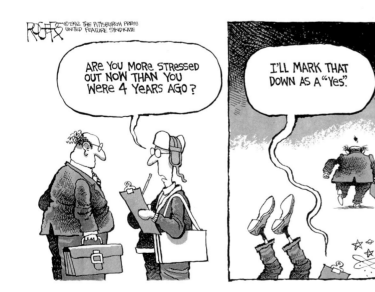

ABOVE LEFT: Some studies can drive a man to drink. *Published 12/21/93.*

ABOVE RIGHT: Or at least give him a reason for not quitting. *Published 01/09/96.*

BELOW: In the end, many studies cancel each other out. *Published 08/23/97.*

17

A CARTOONIST
TAKES UP SMOKING

A CARTOONIST TAKES UP SMOKING

I CAN QUIT ANYTIME

When I was a kid my mom used to send me to the drug store to pick up cigarettes for her. That was before the tobacco industry began targeting children with loveable cartoon spokes-animals. I would usually end up spending the change on chewing gum. Wrigley's was my Philip-Morris. By the time I got to college I was nursing a three-pack-a-day habit. But I never took up smoking, unless you count that one time in 3rd grade.

The kids in my neighborhood had a penchant for forming clubs. One was called "The Top Secret Playboy Club," formed after one of the kids found an old *Playboy* Magazine. We kept it in his garage in a wagon covered with bricks. We met every afternoon to look at it. After a couple of weeks his mom found the magazine and the club disbanded. Another club, even shorter-lived, was the "Smokers Club." Since my mom smoked, I was elected to steal some of her cigarettes for our first official meeting. I grabbed some Winstons from my mom's purse and ran off to meet my friends in our secret, undisclosed location in the woods. After one drag I almost coughed up a lung. It burned so bad I decided to run home and get a cold drink. As I was leaving the woods I glanced back to see a clear trail of smoke rising out of the bushes for all the world (and parents) to see. So much for our undisclosed location. My friends never expressed a desire to reconvene the "Smokers Club." By the time other kids were really taking up the habit, I was over it. I'm sure having a lung doctor for a dad had something to do with that.

Tobacco companies aren't known for their honesty. *Published 05/21/94.*

A FITTING REPLACEMENT FOR JOE CAMEL...

TOBACCO COMPANIES

Non-smokers take their right to breathe very seriously. *Published 05/23/87.*

ABOVE: Smokers were forced out of the workplace. *Published 04/07/94.*

BELOW: Eventually, you couldn't smoke anywhere except in designated areas. *Published 04/08/88.*

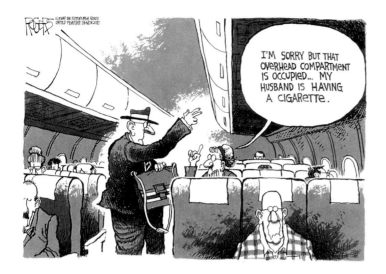

ABOVE LEFT: Airlines discontinued smoking, making some passengers very cranky. *Published 04/26/88.*

ABOVE RIGHT: The rift between smokers and non-smokers was nothing new. *Published 09/24/94.*

MIDDLE LEFT: But the dangers of passive smoke were becoming more evident. *Published 06/12/92.*

MIDDLE RIGHT: The tobacco companies were accused of targeting kids. *Published 06/01/97.*

LEFT: Stores began to crack down on selling cigarettes to minors. *Published 03/31/98.*

18

WHAT WOULD
JESUS DRIVE?

WHAT WOULD JESUS DRIVE?

IT'S NOT EASY TOONING GREEN

What carpenter wouldn't want a tough pickup truck to haul his lumber? My original sketch had Jesus' cross in the bed of the truck. The editors thought that crossed a line and made me take it out. *Published 12/03/02.*

Remember the "crying Indian" commercial from the '70s? I loved that commercial. In retrospect, I wish I could say to him, "dude, we stole your land and wiped out your people and you're crying because of a couple of litterbugs?" At the time, though, it was very moving and definitely influenced my littering habits. Although we may not litter like we used to, we've made up for it in other ways. The forests are being mowed down, toxins are being poured into our air and water, the ozone is rapidly depleting and global warming is causing the polar ice caps to melt. So what do we do? We drive our gas-guzzling SUVs to the polls and elect politicians who care more about industry than the environment. The "crying Indian" wouldn't want the land back now even if we offered it to him.

ABOVE LEFT: We Americans love our SUVs. I used to own one too. But after drawing so many cartoons trashing SUV owners the guilt was getting to me. I traded mine in for a VW. *Published 12/06/03.*

ABOVE RIGHT: We'll do anything to keep our behemoths on wheels. *Published 10/02/97.*

MIDDLE LEFT: Including paying outrageous prices for gas. *Published 05/10/01.*

MIDDLE RIGHT: Fossil fuel has become our most valuable asset. *Published 06/27/00.*

LEFT: It's as American as the flag. *Published 04/04/04.*

ABOVE: You could say we're addicted. *Published 07/05/01.*

BELOW: And how often do we take full advantage of owning an SUV anyway? *Published 05/30/04.*

BUSHES AND TREES

George W. Bush isn't the first President to short-shrift the environment. His dad did a pretty good job of it too. Both Georges are pro-oil, pro-logging and, frankly, pro-any polluting industry that donates enough to their campaigns. Environmental enthusiasts they are not. Here are a few of the cartoons I have drawn over the years about the Bushes and the environment.

ABOVE RIGHT: Bush (41) was cautiously optimistic about pollution. *Published 04/19/90.*

MIDDLE LEFT: Pollute now, ask questions later. *Published 02/21/92.*

MIDDLE RIGHT: National Parks be damned! *Published 09/27/92.*

LEFT: He went to the Earth Summit. I'm still not sure why. *Published 06/16/92.*

ABOVE LEFT: Formerly a Texas oilman, George W. is not a big believer in alternative fuels. *Published 06/8/02.*

ABOVE RIGHT: National Forests be damned! *Published 07/20/04.*

BELOW: Like his father, Bush the younger is a "company man." *Published 06/16/02.*

WHAT, ME WORRY?

What did I do to celebrate the last Earth Day? I made it a point NOT to order takeout in those polystyrene containers. The average American has a lot on his mind: Will I see an end to terrorism in my lifetime? Will social security be there when I retire? Did I set the DVR for *Desperate Housewives*? Stuff like that. It doesn't mean we don't care about the earth's precious resources. It just means we have other priorities. Big companies have other priorities too. In 1989 the *Exxon Valdez* crashed into a reef dumping more than ten million gallons of crude oil into the Prince William Sound off the coast of Alaska. It was the worst oil spill in U.S. history.

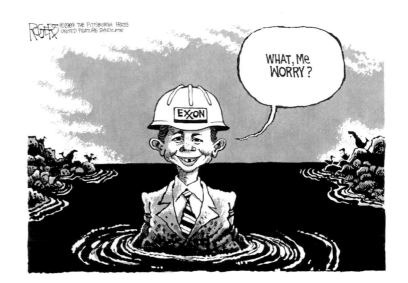

ABOVE RIGHT: Exxon was slow to show any concern about what they had done. *Published 04/06/89.*

MIDDLE LEFT: They were only interested in spinning the story to make themselves look good. *Published 09/01/89.*

MIDDLE RIGHT: The entire coastline turned black. *Published 03/29/89.*

LEFT: In the end, we are still SUV-loving Americans. *Published 11/24/02.*

ABOVE: Between November 1988 and December 1989, there were three major tanker spills dumping over 72 million gallons of crude oil into the world's oceans. *Published 06/28/89.*

MIDDLE: Oil wasn't the only thing washing up. *Published 08/12/88.*

BELOW LEFT: Earth Day is a state of mind. *Published 04/13/90.*

BELOW RIGHT: We may be breathing dirty air ... but it beats the alternative. *Published 07/18/95.*

19

**POP GOES
THE CULTURE**

POP GOES THE CULTURE

TABLOID GAG WRITING

I am an advertising executive's dream. Nobody's more impressed by a clever TV commercial. Nobody's a bigger sucker for a good product tie-in. I walk around humming jingles for fast food, fast cars and fast-acting antacid. I love pop culture. Especially if it includes trends that I know we will be embarrassed to talk about in a few years (i.e., the "Macarena" ... don't deny it, you did it, too). Pop culture makes great cartoon fodder. Sometimes I will make fun of a particular person, issue or trend like Michael Jackson, the O.J. trial or reality TV. More often than that I will draw cartoons using pop culture references to highlight other issues. For instance, during the fall of communism I referenced a famous medical alert commercial. I drew a prostate Lenin statue saying, "I've fallen and I can't get up." Another time I criticized the marketing of cigarettes to kids by showing Joe Camel being replaced by smoking Beanie Babies (remember the Beanie Baby craze?).

I enjoy poking fun at Hollywood's cheesy sentimentality. In 1995 Forrest Gump swept the Oscars despite being up against Pulp Fiction. I couldn't resist knocking Forrest off his park bench. Published 03/28/95.

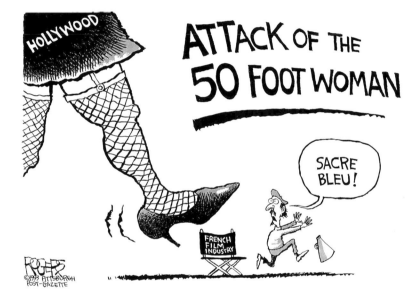

ABOVE LEFT: When the JFK assassination files were made public, I imagined who would be lined up to see them. *Published 08/25/93.*

ABOVE RIGHT: In 1999, I used the popularity of *Stars Wars* to highlight the contrast between U.S. moviegoers and Kosovo refugees. *Published 05/04/99.*

MIDDLE LEFT: In 2003, people lined up for the flu shot. *Published 12/20/03.*

MIDDLE RIGHT: We don't just invade countries with our tanks and soldiers. *Published 12/09/93.*

LEFT: Obnoxious product tie-ins may cause headaches, nausea, and diarrhea. *Published 05/21/05.*

ABOVE: Legacy presidents may cause deficits, war and chaos. *Published 05/22/05.*

BELOW: In recent years, Hollywood has been less than inspired. *Published 06/16/05.*

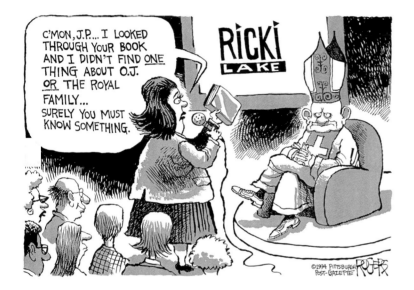

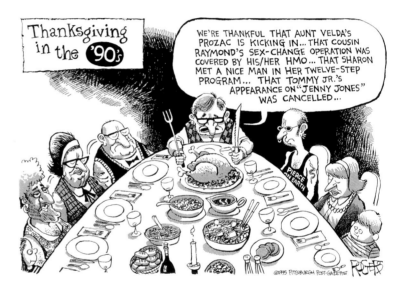

ABOVE LEFT: There will never be another Mister Rogers. *Published 03/02/03.*

ABOVE RIGHT: For that matter, there will never be another comedy like *Seinfeld*. *Published 01/06/98.*

MIDDLE LEFT: Talk shows like *Jerry Springer* and *Ricky Lake* were the precursor to reality TV. *Published 10/25/94.*

MIDDLE RIGHT: They helped normalize family dysfunction. *Published 11/23/95.*

LEFT: Game shows like *The Weakest Link* and *Who Wants to Be a Millionaire?* reinvigorated the game show genre. *Published 04/22/01.*

When David Lynch's *Twin Peaks* hit TV it was all anybody talked about. *Published 05/04/90.*

ABOVE LEFT: Sensationalist TV reporter Geraldo Rivera's autobiography caused a major stir due to revelations of his numerous affairs. *Published 09/20/91.*

ABOVE RIGHT: When Ellen DeGeneres became the first homosexual lead character on primetime television, the ratings went through the roof. *Published 05/04/97.*

MIDDLE LEFT: Janet Jackson's performance at Super Bowl XXXVIII resulted in the wardrobe malfunction heard round the world. It made the FCC nervous. *Published 02/26/05.*

MIDDLE RIGHT: You know we're in trouble when a remake of *The Gong Show* is a hit. *Published 07/24/07.*

LEFT: Viewers can't seem to kick the habit of bad TV. *Published 07/27/07.*

SPORTS NUTS

Some sports fans may not agree that sports are a part of pop culture. They believe sports should be included in the chapter about religion. But this isn't about those people. It's about me. As a kid in the '60s, I dreamed of being Norm Snead, the quarterback of the Philadelphia Eagles. I even had a distinguished career in little league baseball. But I am not a sports fanatic. I couldn't tell you what kind of bat Barry Bonds uses (or what kind of syringe). For me, sports is a front-page story when Madonna sleeps with Dennis Rodman. I follow the scandals and the egos and the insane fans. I may not be able to quote stats like a sports geek, but I love to draw the pop culture of sports.

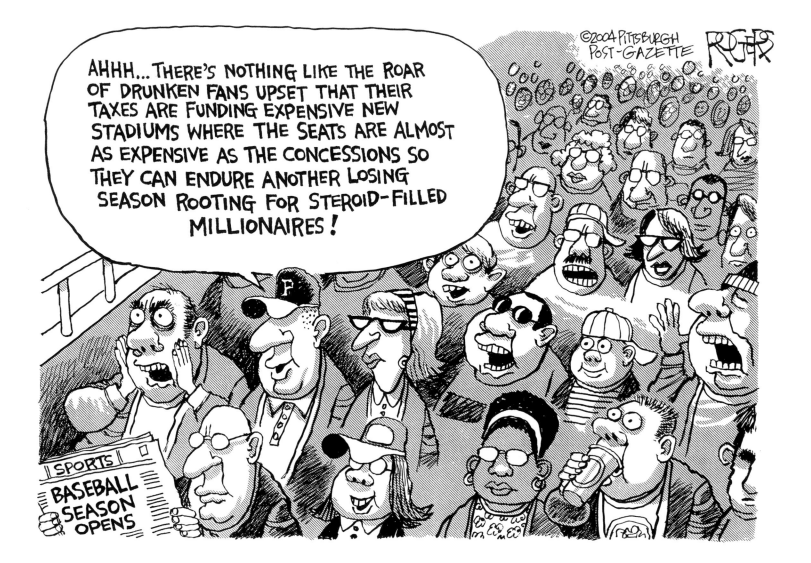

America's pastime has become about more than just baseball. *Published 04/05/04.*

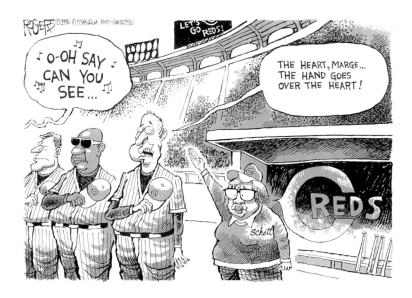

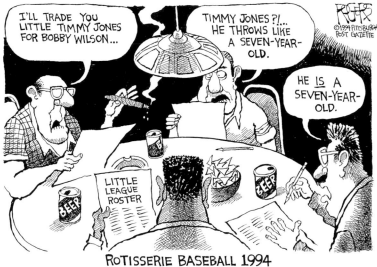

ROTISSERIE BASEBALL 1994

ABOVE LEFT: Baseball is home to all sorts of characters, including Cincinnati Reds' Pete Rose. *Published 01/12/04.*

ABOVE RIGHT: Reds owner Marge Schott was also a real newsmaker. *Published 05/09/96.*

MIDDLE LEFT: A 1994 baseball strike meant fans had to go elsewhere for a fix. *Published 08/30/94.*

MIDDLE RIGHT: Replacement players were used. *Published 03/16/95.*

LEFT: At least we still had little league. *Published 07/18/00.*

ABOVE LEFT: In 2004, baseball got a shot in the arm when America's favorite losers finally won the big one. *Published 10/31/04.*

ABOVE RIGHT: Unfortunately, steroid use has tainted the game. *Published 12/08/04.*

MIDDLE LEFT: Finding out your favorite player is using is like finding out there is no Santa Claus. *Publisehd 12/09/04.*

MIDDLE RIGHT: Congress held hearings on baseball's handling of the steroid scandal. *Published 03/14/04.*

LEFT: Even Bush weighed in. *Published 08/04/05.*

ABOVE: Baseball isn't the only place dealing with a drug scandal. *Published 08/25/04.*

BELOW: Football has been fighting the problem for years. *Published 09/04/88.*

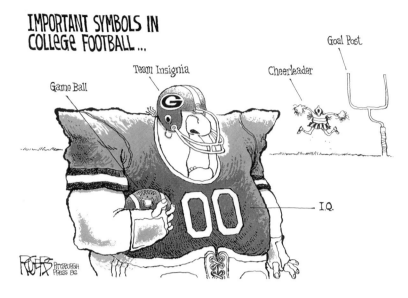

ABOVE LEFT: Many colleges have been criticized for emphasizing sports over academics. *Published 02/16/86.*

ABOVE RIGHT: In the '90s, women made their way into the locker rooms. *Published 10/05/90.*

MIDDLE LEFT: Some think deer hunting is a sport. The deer don't find it very sporting. *Published 12/01/88.*

MIDDLE RIGHT: Tonya Harding's attack on Nancy Kerrigan turned figure skating into a full contact sport. *Published 01/18/94.*

LEFT: In 1996, a North Carolina first-grader made headlines when his school accused him of sexual harassment for kissing a classmate. At the same time Baltimore Orioles second baseman, Roberto Alomar, received very little punishment for spitting in the face of an umpire. *Published 10/05/96.*

ABOVE: When Mike Tyson bit Evander Holyfield's ear, the boxing world was shocked and offended. *Published 07/01/97.*

BELOW: But not that shocked and offended. *Published 07/12/97.*

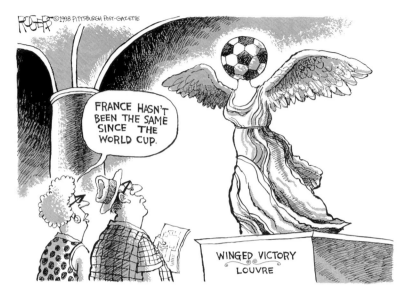

ABOVE LEFT: Tyson's comeback was a disappointment. *Published 08/04/04.*

ABOVE RIGHT: In 1998, France won their first World Cup. *Published 07/16/98..*

MIDDLE LEFT: In 1999, the U.S. won the Women's World Cup. *Published 07/13/99.*

MIDDLE RIGHT: In the final game, Brandi Chastain kicked a goal and then celebrated by taking off her jersey. Her sports bra became a topic of conversation. *Published 08/01/99.*

LEFT: The U.S. women went on to win gold in the 2004 Olympics. *Published 08/28/04.*

ABOVE LEFT: Beach Volleyball also became a big hit with a gold medal performance by the U.S. Women's team. *Published 09/08/04.*

ABOVE RIGHT: If TV Olympic coverage is to be believed, the tragic stories of the athletes is as important as their performances. *Published 09/28/00.*

MIDDLE LEFT: 2004 marked the fiftieth anniversary of Roger Bannister's sub-four minute mile. *Published 05/05/04.*

MIDDLE RIGHT: It was also the year without professional hockey. *Published 11/10/04.*

LEFT: Fantasy leagues have grown in popularity. *Published 09/29/04.*

In the end, it's important to remember it's only a game. *Published 01/26/05.*

ABOVE LEFT: Michael Vick, quarterback for the Atlanta Falcons, was convicted of hosting illegal dog fights in his back yard. When the dogs failed to perform well, they were killed. *Published 08/23/07.*

ABOVE RIGHT: Barry Bonds couldn't shake the accusations of steroid use. *Published 11/22/07.*

BELOW LEFT: Steroids — it's what's for breakfast. *Published 12/20/07.*

BELOW RIGHT: Terrell Owens of the Dallas cowboys teared up when his team didn't make the playoffs. When Hillary Clinton teared up during the primaries, she won New Hampshire. *Published 01/15/08.*

THE CULT OF PERSONALITY

Americans love people who are bigger than life. We love to follow the strange and sometimes tragic lives of people who become stars. When the rich and famous fall on hard times, it makes us feel better about our own miserable lives. Often, the thing that makes them famous isn't the thing that makes them infamous. OJ made his name in football and movies long before he became the world's most famous murder suspect. Michael Jackson didn't start his career as a suspected pedophile. Martha Stewart only trades illegally as a hobby.

ABOVE RIGHT: Michael Jackson was caught on tape dangling his baby over a hotel balcony railing. *Published 11/23/02.*

MIDDLE LEFT: Jackson's idiosyncrasies can provide good material for parody. *Published 06/18/05.*

MIDDLE RIGHT: A question to the parents who let their kids sleep over at Jackson's ranch: What the %#@$ were you thinking? *Published 11/27/03.*

LEFT: The world was shocked when, after a five-month child molestation trial, Michael Jackson was acquitted. *Published 06/14/05.*

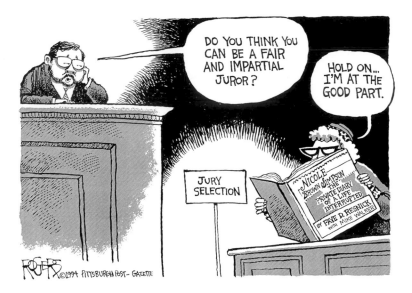

ABOVE LEFT: It was almost as if the O.J. Trial even had God distracted. *Published 02/02/95.*

ABOVE RIGHT: Faye Resnick wrote a book about her murdered friend, Nicole. *Published 10/22/94.*

RIGHT: She wasn't the only one. Everybody had a book including one from a psychic and one from a journalist called *Raging Heart*. *Published 02/05/95.*

BELOW: The media took the center ring as usual. *Published 06/23/94.*

Even Judge Ito couldn't prevent the circus atmosphere. *Published 10/09/94.*

EVOLUTION OF THE NEWS MEDIA...

ABOVE LEFT: Tabloid journalism was quickly becoming the rule as opposed to the exception. *Published 07/17/94.*

ABOVE RIGHT: O.J. may have gotten away with murder, but he was still finding it hard to get work. *Published 02/11/97.*

MIDDLE LEFT: The justice system still works from time to time. *Published 06/05/97.*

MIDDLE RIGHT: In 1995, faced with the threat of more bombings, *The Washington Post* and *The New York Times* agreed to print the "Unabomber Manifesto." *Published 09/23/95.*

LEFT: Unabomber Ted Kaczynski insisted on being his own lawyer. He could have used Johnnie Cochran. *Published 01/11/98.*

ABOVE LEFT: In 1994 it was revealed that both Prince Charles and Lady Diana were having affairs. *Published 10/15/94.*

ABOVE RIGHT: The world mourned when Diana died in a car crash in Paris. *Published 09/02/97.*

BELOW: Initially, the paparazzi were blamed for her death. *Published 09/04/97.*

THE ETERNAL MEDIA

THE EVOLUTION of USING UNNAMED SOURCES...

A TALE of TWO CASES of MYOPIC ZEAL...

ABOVE LEFT: JFK Jr.'s untimely death reinforced the media's fascination with the "Kennedy Curse." *Published 07/22/99.*

ABOVE RIGHT: The media's reputation has been severely damaged in recent years by increased plagiarism, unreliable sources and even invented stories like those by *The New York Times'* Jason Blair. *Published 06/02/05.*

MIDDLE LEFT: Dan Rather's blunder with forged memos about Bush's National Guard service didn't help any. His departure signaled an end to an era of network anchor news. *Published 11/25/04.*

MIDDLE RIGHT: The media is held up to a different kind of integrity than politicians. *Published 01/15/05.*

LEFT: Gone are the heady days of Watergate journalism. *Published 06/05/05.*

ABOVE: Martha Stewart proved to be a savvy businesswoman. *Published 10/21/99.*

BELOW: Prison seemed to suit her. She came out looking great with a new TV show. *Published 03/11/04.*

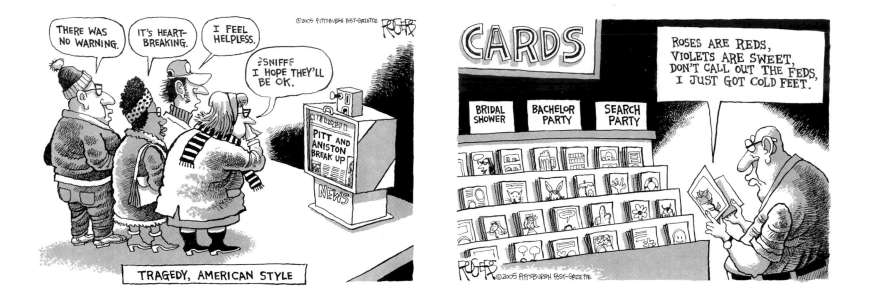

ABOVE LEFT: While most of the world worried about the victims of a devastating tsunami, we were dealing with a different kind of loss. *Published 01/13/05.*

ABOVE RIGHT: A runaway bride in Georgia angered the public by turning her wedding jitters into a nationwide search and rescue operation. *Published 05/03/05.*

BELOW: Tom Cruise, seen by some as a scientologist nut case, publicly declared his love for actress Katie Holmes by jumping up and down on Oprah's couch. *Published 07/10/05.*

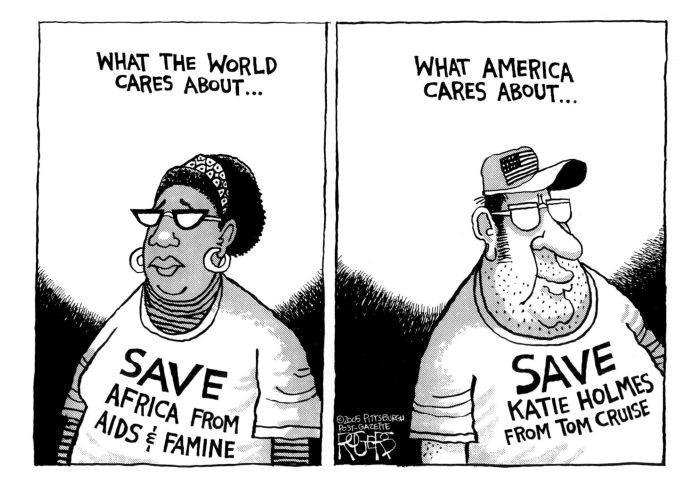

ABOVE: Rehab became a trendy way to excuse any and all behavior. *Published 02/08/07.*

BELOW LEFT: Anna Nicole Smith's death became a never-ending story. *Published 02/23/07.*

BELOW RIGHT: Oprah's ongoing weight problem continued to captivate audiences everywhere. *Published 12/12/08.*

20

DON'T SHOOT, I'M JUST THE CARTOONIST

DON'T SHOOT, I'M JUST THE CARTOONIST

GUNS DRAWN

I grew up a red-blooded, GI Joe-toting, cowboy and indians-playing, cap gun-loving, '60s American boy. My favorite TV dramas, like *Man From Uncle*, *Wild, Wild West*, *Mission Impossible*, and *Mod Squad* featured pistol-packing detectives, cowboys and spies. My favorite movies were those Spaghetti Westerns starring Clint Eastwood like *The Good, the Bad and the Ugly*. They contained very little dialogue but lots of action-packed gunfights with hard-boiled leading men. Nobody was cooler than Clint as he squinted against the sun, puffed on that cigar and threw his poncho over his shoulder to free up his shooting arm.

My job as a cartoonist has forced me to step away from the TV and turn a critical eye to the reality of guns and violence. Granted, Hollywood would be pretty boring without guns, but actual gunplay is far more tragic. Every year, more than 30,000 people are shot to death in murders, suicides and accidents. Our schools have become battlegrounds. Guns have turned our inner cities into war zones. Congress is too addicted to the gun lobby's money to pass tough gun legislation. And organizations like the National Rifle Association (NRA) put gun ownership above human life.

My message to the NRA? I'll give up drawing anti-gun cartoons when they pry my pen from my cold dead hand! Until then I will squint against the sun, puff on a cigar and throw my poncho over my shoulder to free up my drawing arm.

WHICH OF THESE IS MORE LIKELY TO BE BANNED?

In 1992, when several boys were shot because their high-powered super soakers were mistaken for real guns, brave legislators were quick to suggest a ban on squirt guns. *Published 06/11/92.*

SHOOTS AND KILLS OVER 22,000 PEOPLE A YEAR

SHOOTS WATER

Guns are the new school supplies. *Published 11/19/94.*

ABOVE: They've replaced the old weapons of choice. *Published 03/28/98.*

BELOW: In 1999, when the Columbine school shooting occurred, some people blamed the movie, *The Matrix*, and its trench coat-wearing heroes. *Published 04/25/99.*

ABOVE LEFT: Some people blamed the parents. *Published 04/29/99.*

ABOVE RIGHT: Some people blamed the schools and teachers for not seeing the signs. *Published 03/11/01.*

MIDDLE LEFT: Speaking of not seeing the signs. *Published 08/21/99.*

MIDDLE RIGHT: Some parents actually do try to reign in their kids. *Published 07/04/93.*

BELOW LEFT: Some parents are just absent. *Published 04/28/98.*

ABOVE: Some parents should have their heads examined. Did I just sound like my dad? *Published 03/27/98.*

BELOW: Suddenly, parents are worried about their kids being bullied or becoming outcasts. *Published 04/27/99.*

The National Rifle Association thinks everyone should be armed. *Published 01/24/89.*

ABOVE LEFT: They protect the rights of weekend sportsmen to own assault weapons. *Published 03/19/89.*

ABOVE RIGHT: In 1999 Amadou Diallo was shot 41 times by police on the doorstep of his Bronx home. They said they thought his wallet was a gun. *Published 04/08/00.*

MIDDLE LEFT: The GOP is more worried about sinful Hollywood than too many guns on the streets. *Published 06/09/95.*

BELOW LEFT: They are compassionate when it comes to gun ownership. *Published 06/26/99.*

BELOW RIGHT: NRA president Charlton Heston was critical of Clinton's gun policies. *Published 06/11/98.*

ABOVE: Bush brought the NRA back to the White House. *Published 03/13/01.*

BELOW: He's helped bring the NRA out of their shell. *Published 10/17/02.*

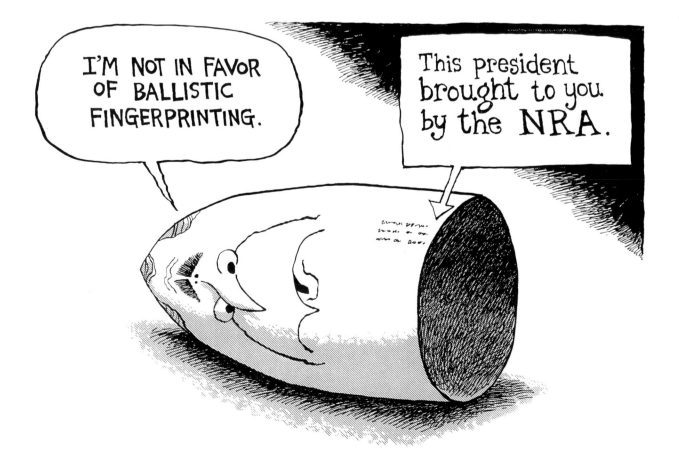

ABOVE: Congress can't seem to loosen the NRA's death grip. *Published 10/25/05.*

BELOW: And so the tragic love affair continues... *Published 04/19/07.*

21

LAND OF THE WHITE, HOME OF THE STRAIGHT

LAND OF THE WHITE, HOME OF THE STRAIGHT

DISCRIMINATING CARTOONS

There's a song in the Tony Award-winning musical *Avenue Q* called "Everyone's A Little Bit Racist." It's a hilarious song. Not just because it's sung by muppets, but because it's true. Everybody IS a little bit racist. We just don't like to talk about it. Another uncomfortable but funny song in the show states, "if you were gay that'd be OK … I mean, 'cause, hey, I'd like you anyway."

America has come a long way in the battle for tolerance and racial equality, but we still have a ways to go. After all, we still live in a country where African Americans in Texas are dragged behind pickup trucks and gays in Wyoming are beaten to death.

In a way, this country was founded on racism.
Published 10/13/91.

ABOVE LEFT: In 1995, the country was still reeling from the O.J. verdict. Louis Farrakhan's past anti-Semitic and racist comments managed to taint his otherwise noble "Million Man March." At the same time, the Atlanta Braves were facing the Cleveland Indians in the World Series. *Published 10/19/95.*

ABOVE RIGHT: In 1987, Austrian President Kurt Waldheim was banned from the U.S. because of his ties to German atrocities in WW II. *Published 04/30/87.*

MIDDLE LEFT: Clinton struggled with what to do about similar atrocities in Bosnia. *Published 05/11/93.*

MIDDLE RIGHT: Then came Kosovo. *Published 10/08/98.*

LEFT: Our growing Latino population is also battling against discrimination. *Published 06/06/98.*

ABOVE: Affirmative action is society's way of atoning for the sins of the past. *Published 03/14/95.*

BELOW: Some Republicans, like George H. W. Bush, don't think there's anything to atone for. *Published 06/29/89.*

ABOVE LEFT: "Quotas" are an evil concept in Republican circles. *Published 10/23/90.*

ABOVE RIGHT: Meanwhile, Michael Jackson tried to sing about racial issues while his skin turned paler and paler. *Published 11/22/91.*

MIDDLE LEFT: The GOP is only frightened by racism when it makes them look bad, like when David Duke entered the '92 presidential race. *Published 12/06/91.*

MIDDLE RIGHT: In 1992, a mostly white jury acquitted four police officers accused in the videotaped beating of Rodney King. The verdict triggered the LA riots. *Published 05/01/92.*

LEFT: In 1994, Disney proposed building "Disney's America," a history theme park, on historic Civil War battlefields in Virginia. It would have included the depiction of life on the Southern plantation. How quaint. *Published 07/05/94.*

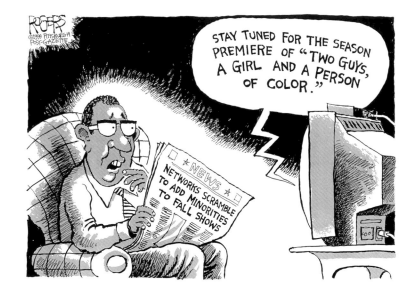

ABOVE LEFT: Also in 1994, Denny's restaurant was found guilty of racial discrimination. *Published 05/28/94.*

ABOVE RIGHT: *The Bell Curve,* a controversial book addressing race and intelligence, was published the same year. *Published 10/23/94.*

MIDDLE LEFT: In 1996, Texaco was hit with a big anti-discrimination lawsuit. *Published 11/14/96.*

MIDDLE RIGHT: Criticized for not having enough non-whites in prime time, the networks began adding roles for minorities. *Published 10/02/99.*

LEFT: Sure, people like the late Supreme Court Justice Thurgood Marshall have made some progress. *Published 01/26/93.*

Real equality is an uphill battle. *Published 09/28/97.*

ABOVE LEFT: In 1998, three white men in Jasper, Texas, dragged a black man to death behind a pickup truck. *Published 02/25/99.*

ABOVE RIGHT: Despite advances in civil rights, we still have battles over the Confederate flag. *Published 01/22/00.*

MIDDLE LEFT: We still have racial profiling. *Published 04/19/01.*

MIDDLE RIGHT: We still have racist politicians in positions of power. *Published 12/22/02.*

LEFT: And we still haven't atoned for the whole slavery thing. *Published 03/26/02.*

DON'T ASK, DON'T TELL

The battle to secure equal rights for gays and lesbians has been called the new civil rights movement. Unfortunately, most Americans believe they're praying to a deity who likes the ladies (i.e., God's a hetero). In this country, tolerance for alternative lifestyles is about as popular as a Rob Schneider movie. In 2004, Bush even managed to make gay weddings look scarier to voters than Osama bin Laden, and easier to smoke out.

The eighties introduced us to the AIDS crisis.
Published 06/03/87.

1988 Campaign Front-Runner

AIDS

ABOVE LEFT: Free love was out, condoms were in. *Published 02/12/87.*

ABOVE RIGHT: A decade after AIDS surfaced the government was criticized for not spending enough on finding a cure. *Published 12/02/93.*

MIDDLE LEFT: Critics accused Bush of not making AIDS a priority. *Published 12/04/03.*

MIDDLE RIGHT: Gays have never felt welcome in the U.S. military. *Published 07/26/93.*

LEFT: The "don't ask, don't tell" policy didn't eliminate discrimination. *Published 05/13/93.*

ABOVE: The Tailhook scandal and several other military sex scandals made the gay issue seem like small potatoes. *Published 11/17/96.*

BELOW LEFT: The U.S. military isn't the only group of men in uniform who don't encourage alternative lifestyles. *Published 07/17/01.*

BELOW RIGHT: There is no "gay outreach" merit badge. *Published 07/06/00.*

Capitol Hill isn't gay-friendly either. *Published 09/15/96.*

ABOVE LEFT: In fact, they can be downright unfriendly. *Published 04/29/03.*

ABOVE RIGHT: Especially a certain late senator from North Carolina. *Published 07/11/95.*

BELOW: Matthew Shepard found out how some people in Wyoming feel about gays. *Published 10/15/98.*

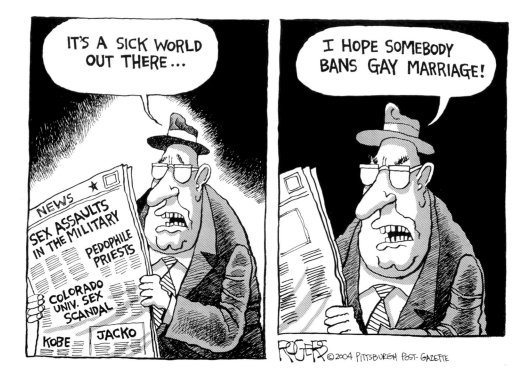

ABOVE LEFT: Rush Limbaugh tried a short-lived stint as a sportscaster. He didn't give up his day job, radio hatemonger. *Published 07/20/03.*

ABOVE RIGHT: In 2003, the Supreme Court invalidated the anti-sodomy law in Texas. *Published 07/01/03.*

MIDDLE: Equality for gays is still a controversial idea to many Americans. *Published 03/13/04.*

LEFT: George W. Bush even turned gay marriage into an issue in the 2004 campaign. *Published 02/21/04.*

22

SACRED COW
TIPPING

SACRED COW TIPPING

HOLY SACRILEGE, BATMAN!

When the Pope came to the States he chastised U.S. Catholics who disagreed with his conservative policies.
Published 08/12/93.

Some people think that there are special entities like popes, presidents and religious icons that are "off limits" when it comes to criticism or satire. I don't believe in "sacred cows." While I would never target someone just for their beliefs, if those beliefs are used as a cloak for abuse of power or civil rights violations, then all bets are off. My cartoons critical of the Catholic Church's policies and scandals have earned me scathing mentions in assorted church bulletins, angry letters to the editor and even a reprimand in the Vatican newsletter. The church doesn't have much of a sense of humor. I should know. I grew up Catholic. It doesn't matter if it's religion, patriotism, capital punishment or abortion. If I see a self-righteous, fear-mongering demagogue standing in a field, I'll tip him over.

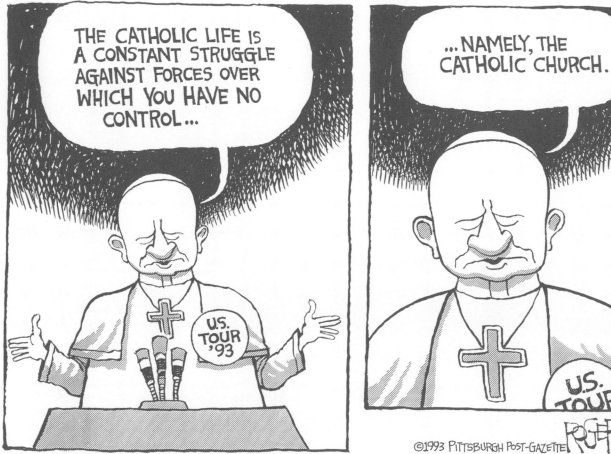

ABOVE LEFT: When Castro had an audience with the Pope I couldn't resist the parallels. *Published 01/20/98.*

ABOVE RIGHT: The Church spent decades covering up their pedophile priest scandal. *Published 04/06/02.*

MIDDLE LEFT: Rather than deal with the crimes, they just moved the pedophiles from one hiding place to another. *Published 04/21/02.*

MIDDLE RIGHT: Saint Jude, the patron saint of lost causes, could never have imagined this. *Published 03/23/02.*

BELOW LEFT: The Boston diocese, under Cardinal Bernard Law, was responsible for covering up one of the worst pedophile priest scandals in church history. At the same time, the popular "Iraq's Most Wanted" playing cards were fast becoming a collector's item. *Published 07/26/03.*

ABOVE: Rome tried to draw attention to the "sins" of gay marriage instead. *Published 08/05/03.*

BELOW: Finally, Cardinal Law resigned. *Published 12/19/02.*

ABOVE LEFT: If only all religious leaders had the humility and grace of Mother Teresa. *Published 09/09/07.*

ABOVE RIGHT: In 2004 Mel Gibson came out with his controversial film about the final days of Christ. *Published 02/19/04.*

MIDDLE LEFT: Despite being criticized for being anti-Semitic and extremely gory, it made a fortune at the box office. *Published 03/20/04.*

MIDDLE RIGHT: Catholics aren't alone when it comes to scandal. In the eighties, televangelist Jim Bakker was caught having an affair with Jessica Hahn. *Published 02/23/88.*

BELOW LEFT: Bakker was later indicted on federal charges of fraud, tax evasion and racketeering. *Published 10/07/01.*

POLITICS BEGIN AT CONCEPTION

You can't talk about religion and politics without mentioning abortion and the death penalty. Both are very highly charged issues with sharply divided emotional arguments and organized lobbying efforts. Both issues, when addressed in cartoons, generate a lot of mail and phone calls. With the addition of controversial issues like stem cell research and frozen embryos, you've got enough material to draw something every day of the week if you wanted to. Needless to say, my editors don't want me to.

ABOVE: When anti-abortion extremists gun down abortion doctors, it doesn't help promote the "pro-life" message. *Published 03/13/93.*

ABOVE LEFT: Killing kind of goes against the "Christian" message. *Published 08/02/94.*

ABOVE RIGHT: Politicians are not above using the abortion issue to their political advantage. *Published 07/08/93.*

MIDDLE LEFT: Especially during an election year. *Published 04/03/04.*

MIDDLE RIGHT: Conservatives are still hoping the Supreme Court will overturn "Roe v Wade." *Published 07/05/89.*

BELOW LEFT: Surrogate mothers are a blessing to infertile couples, but sometimes there can be complications. *Published 02/04/87.*

ABOVE: You take the house and the minivan, I'll keep the kidsicles. *Published 08/09/89.*

BELOW: Scientific advances have changed the debate. *Published 07/21/01.*

ABOVE LEFT: Conservatives have rushed to the aid of these yet-to-be-thawed-out voters. *Published 08/16/01.*

ABOVE RIGHT: The possible benefits of stem cell research are worth praying for. *Published 05/26/05.*

MIDDLE LEFT: During his six years as governor of Texas, George W. Bush presided over 152 executions including the first woman put to death in Texas since the Civil War. *Published 02/10/98.*

MIDDLE RIGHT: In 2004, the only countries that executed more people than the U.S. were China, Iran and Viet Nam. *Published 05/13/04.*

BELOW LEFT: Prior to Timothy McVeigh's execution, a public debate emerged over whether executions should be televised or not. *Published 05/13/01.*

ABOVE: When the D.C. sniper was caught, the real sniping began. *Published 11/12/02.*

BELOW LEFT: When Terri Schiavo's feeding tube was removed in Florida, the usual suspects showed up. *Published 04/03/05.*

BELOW RIGHT: With a "culture of life" like this, who needs death? *Published 10/14/00.*

EXPLETIVES TO
THE EDITOR

Cartooning is a give-and-take process. I GIVE the readers something to think about … and they TAKE the opportunity to practice all the curse words they've ever learned. Most of this "practice" (some readers are not practicing, they're real pros) takes the form of angry letters and emails. There are a few distinct types of letter writers. I have names for them:

1. TAGGERS: "Tagging" is what graffiti artists do to bridges, buildings and subway cars. They leave their mark. My taggers tear the cartoon out of the paper and adorn it with their signature mark. It's not uncommon to see the words "F**K YOU!" scrawled across the cartoon in magic marker. Sometimes taggers get creative and change balloon text, but they almost never include an accompanying letter or a return address.

2. STATERS: Staters are the ones who write to me from state mental institutions and prisons. Their letters are usually made up of crooked lines of tiny, naïve looking handwriting that fills up the entire page including the margins. One stater sent three handwritten pages in which each letter of every word was rendered with a different colored pencil. I was impressed with his dedication to craft. The letter was incomprehensible but pretty.

3. NOVELISTS: These are the ones who write enough to make up an entire book. Some are autobiographies, starting with "when I was young a cup of coffee cost a nickel, everyone had respect for the president and there were no homosexuals …." Others write compendiums of history containing more citations than a grad school thesis. The only upside to reading one of these novels is knowing the writer will be crushed when their carefully crafted literature is edited to a couple of sentences for the letters page.

4. SPOILERS: These are the people who send well-written, intelligent, thought-provoking letters but then spoil it all by adding "P.S. Go to hell, you liberal A**HOLE!"

When I drew an editorial cartoon about the 60th anniversary of the Hiroshima atomic bomb, the fallout of letters, emails and phone calls was pretty heavy. I explained to one WW II veteran caller that I wasn't calling our brave military men and women terrorists. I told him the 60th anniversary was a chance to pause and reflect on whether or not we needed to drop two nuclear weapons that killed hundreds of thousands of civilians to end the war? I think it is a valid question to ask, especially in the context of today's new "war on terror." He paused for a moment, and then said, "I don't agree, and as long as I have you on the phone, I want to complain about another cartoon you drew. What kind of idiot would depict our president as a monkey?"

May 7, 1994

Cartoonist Rob Rogers
Pittsburgh Post-Gazette
Pittsburgh, PA. 15200

Your cartoon, "The Vatican Approves Altar Girls" which appeared in the Phila. Inquirer of May 1, 1994.

Sir:

This cartoon attack on us Catholics reminds me of the Nazi Kulturkampf against German Catholics in the 1930s which exceeded in violence Bismarck's earlier Kulturkampf. I may call your attention to some easily available instances of Nazi rage, cool style or warm, against Catholics, although for a more complete story one should consult the contemporary literature, especially that of European countries, with its description of antiCatholic cartoons, parades, posters, handbills, pamphlets, plays, movies, books, newspapers, magazines, etc.

a. Albert Speer's "Inside the Third Reich", Avon, 1971, p. 155, states that Hitler used to engage in "endless tirades on The Catholic Church".

b. Joachim Fest in "Hitler", Vintage, 1975, said Hitler would rage on "marching into the Vatican", p. 497, to clean out that "herd of swine", "that rabble", p. 669, in their "insipid Christian heaven", p. 692, and "hang the Pope", p. 689.

c. Robert Payne, "The Life and Death of Adolf Hitler", Pop. Lib., 1973, says that Hitler "raved against the Church" as early as 1911, and criticized it as "bringing in corrupt influences", pp. 91, 298, 302.

d. Willi Frischauer's "The Rise and Fall of Hermann Goering", Ballantine, 1951, says Goering "fulminated against the Vatican", pp. 42-3, made "frequent attacks on the Catholic Church", p. 85, and referred to Catholics as "black ravens", pp. 121-2. Hitler used the expression "black crows".

e. Walter Schellenberg in "Hitler's Secret Service", Jove, 1977, says that he attacked the Church as did Heinrich Himmler, Joseph Goebbels, and Martin Bormann, and further that Hitler planned to "deport the Pope to Avignon", pp. 20-22, 302, 362.

f. "The Goebbels Diaries", Lochner ed., 1948, has many attacks, as note pp/ ix, 13, 17, 40, 83, 110, 113, 140, 159, 163, 234, 239, 270, 400, 408, including slams at the hierarchy as the "most loathsome riff-raff next to the Jews", p. 168, "the Pope

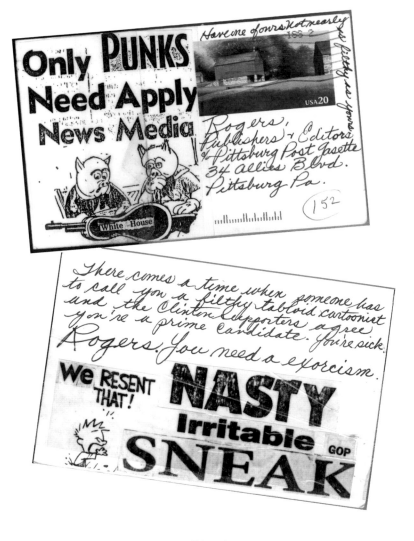

ABOVE LEFT: NOVELIST EXAMPLE — This writer compares me to the Third Reich and then goes on to cite everything written about Hitler.

ABOVE RIGHT: STATER EXAMPLE 1 — I nicknamed this writer "Pig Boy" because he loved to paste cartoon pigs on all his postcards. Pig Boy thought I was a Clinton-hating right-winger. He was clearly disturbed.

BELOW: TAGGER EXAMPLE 1 — I got my homework back with a helpful critique and a passing grade. Thanks, professor!

April 21, 2005

Mr. Tom Waseleski
Editorial Page Editor
Pittsburgh Post Gazette
34 Boulevard of the Allies
Pittsburgh, PA 15222

Re: Pope bashing

Mr. Waseleski,

You evidently cannot understand that Roman Catholicism is a religion, not a club. What you think about "a more modern approach" is irrelevant. "Liberal Catholics" are self-centered individuals who believe that any element of Church teaching or tradition should be changed to meet what they want. Each one believes that they are the center of the universe. Locally, they can always join Bill Hausen in Sewickley or, start their own church.

Your cartoonist, Rob Rogers has spent much of his career attacking the Catholic religion. He is a low-life asshole, and I am sick of him. Is it any wonder that your paper is commonly known as the Putz-Gazette? It is because of the editorial page. I refuse to have the P-G make another nickel from me. Please cancel my subscription immediately.

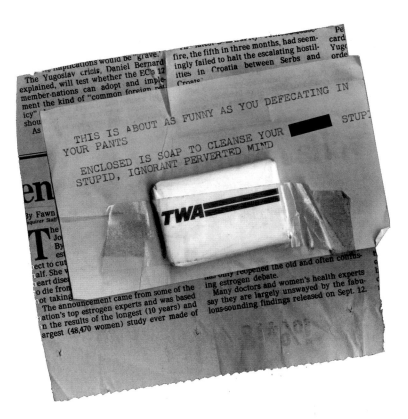

ABOVE LEFT: SPOILER EXAMPLE — This Catholic was making a perfectly sensible argument until he spoiled it by calling me a nasty name. What would the Pope say?

ABOVE RIGHT: STATER EXAMPLE 2 — This fan taped a bar of soap to the back of one of my cartoons. Let me get this straight, the airlines can't keep track of my luggage but they have time to make soap?

BELOW: TAGGER EXAMPLE 2 — "Smart Alek" was by far the nicest thing I was ever called.

Here are some recent "letters to the editor" regarding my cartoons.
The letters have been edited for length and only include the writer's first name
and neighborhood or township.

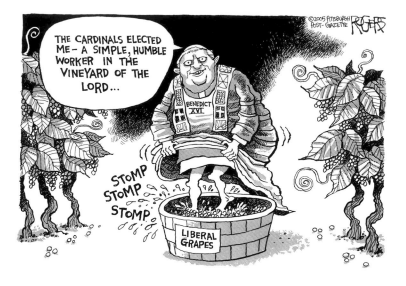

Published 04/21/05.

April 10, 2005

It's hard to make a cartoon insulting and ignorant. Yet Rob Rogers managed to do both on April 7. It was insulting in its timing. Hundreds of thousands of pilgrims were still patiently waiting in Rome's streets to view the body of the late Pope John Paul II on the morning the PG published this cartoon. The pope's Mass of Christian Burial had not yet been celebrated. Where is the cartoonist's (and the editors') common decency? It insulted the leaders of the Catholic Church. Put church teachings up in smoke, with a flick of a Bic? It even insulted liberals, and their nuanced understanding of how the church's teachings may evolve over time.

—Frank, Mount Oliver

April 26, 2005

Let's all check our watches. By my reckoning it took Rob Rogers just 48 hours, give or take, to produce an insulting editorial caricature of the views of Pope Benedict XVI. Showing the Holy Father stomping on undefined "liberal grapes", Rogers evidences no knowledge of where the Holy Father might stand on any number of issues ... Give him a little time, Mr. Rogers—and do a little investigation—before you reaffirm your biases publicly.

—David, McCandless

May 1, 2005

To the right of your tenuous welcome to Pope Benedict was Rob Rogers' expected and weak attempt to amuse your readers at the expense of an easy target. From what I've heard about Pope Benedict from those who know him better than your cartoonist, he will use the sour grapes gathered by the liberals to make a sweet wine with which he will gladden the hearts of the needy, the downtrodden and the forgotten.

—Helen, North Versailles

TRUST ME... YOUR FEEDING TUBE WILL BE PUT TO BETTER USE THIS WAY!

SOCIAL SECURITY

WALL ST.

©2005 PITTSBURGH POST-GAZETTE

Published 03/29/05.

April 4, 2005

... But even granting the wide latitude given the PG drawing staff to craft distorted messages, surely some code of cartoonist's ethics draws a line beyond which the opinion expressed insults our basic humanity. That line was crossed by Rob Rogers' March 29 editorial cartoon in which Terri Schiavo's condition was cruelly contorted to portray President Bush inserting a "Social Security" feeding tube into "Wall Street" rather than an elderly benefits recipient. Our shared humanity cries out for the cartoonist's apology or censure or termination.

— Arthur, Churchill

Published 05/14/05.

May 24, 2005

Respect them

I am not one to write letters to newspapers, but Rob Rogers' editorial cartoon on May 14—depicting a military recruiter as a stereotypical slick used car salesman standing next to a hearse—went so far beyond the pale I have to respond. In a few months I will be transitioning into the civilian sector after 24 years active duty service in the U.S. Navy. Your unfortunate cartoon derides that sense of duty and those who have sacrificed so much so that Americans can enjoy the freedoms we hold so dear. In the future I ask that your paper respect and admire the soldiers, sailors, airmen and marines who are willing to serve the greater good, their sacrifice and their dedication to duty.

—Herb, Indiana Township

May 28, 2005

As I read your fine newspaper on May 14, I was shocked to see the cartoon on your editorial page by Rob Rogers. The cartoonist's insensitivity for a very admirable military occupation is deplorable. Mr. Rogers, the military is a lot more than the Iraq war. Let us respect our military personnel and thank them for the job they do. Above all, let us show respect for those who have made the ultimate sacrifice. You owe them and their families a sincere apology.

—Richard, Pottstown

Published 04/27/04.

Dear Sir,

I was appalled when I came across your cartoon showing your take on the President's views of terrorists and abortion activists. The similarity is that both groups kill innocents (and you can't be more innocent than an unborn child) with no remorse. Your cartoon was repugnant.

—William, Edina, MN

Published 08/09/05.

August 10, 2005

Regarding yesterday's editorial cartoon by Rob Rogers, showing a little boy on his father's lap, watching an image of the Hiroshima mushroom cloud on TV and saying, "Which terrorist group did that?" The palpable stupidity of Rogers' likening Hiroshima to today's terrorism should be, but is not, an embarrassment to any thinking person. The editors should not be pleased with what passes as provocative thought on the editorial pages of their paper. If there is a more primitive mind than Mr. Rogers' published in the leading paper of a sizeable U.S. city, I'd be amazed.

—John, Pine

August 10, 2005

The inane comparison of our use of the atomic bomb to end the war in the Pacific with terrorism is a sad reflection of the tragic state of education in this country, and more importantly the collective short attention span of the society we've become. Anyone with even the most basic grasp of history (or the combination of the ability to read and a little initiative) knows that comparing cowardly, modern-day terrorism to nation-states at war is specious at best and idiotic at worst. In the name of all that is holy, people, crack open a damn book once in a while.

—Thomas, McCandless

August 15, 2005

Rob Rogers' Aug. 9 cartoon is an uninformed insult to the crews of the Enola Gay and Bock's Car, the B-29 bombers that dropped the atom bombs on Japan. To label these brave crewmen as terrorists indicates an abysmal ignorance of the situation. The carnage wrought by the two bombs was appalling, but still the lesser of two evils. I flew 71 missions as a bomber pilot in World War II and have never considered myself a terrorist.

—Charles, Crafton

Most Letters are born out of anger, but once in a blue moon a reader comes to my defense.

August 28, 2005

Rob Rogers notes in his PostScript column "When a Cartoon Is Worth a Thousand Words (of Abuse)" (Aug. 21 Forum) that he's often accused of intentionally picking fights with his editorial cartoons. Well, let's hope so. The best art is supposed to roust us out of intellectual lethargy. Howling at art – in rage or in glee – is good!

A few years ago the Pulitzer Prize committee thought enough of his work to choose Rogers as a finalist. It's people like Rogers who are helping to put our city on the cultural map.

If you hate his stuff, go ahead and throw tantrums and cancel subscriptions. That's your right. Just as it's his to draw extremely funny and sharply pointed editorial cartoons.

—Mary, West End

KILLED CARTOONS

When readers react to my cartoons about the pope or George Bush or the war, it's nice to know the paper has my back. After all, it is often one of the editors whom the angry reader wants to speak to, not me. I am lucky to work for editors (and a publisher) who value tough sometimes biting, editorial cartoons and have the courage to use them. Not all newspapers are like that; not all readers are so well-served.

Before one of my cartoons ever sees the light of day, it has to pass muster with my editorial page editor. Most days he's there to help me with clarity or to save me from embarrassing punctuation, but every now and then he kills a cartoon. It doesn't happen often, but since my job is to push boundaries, it's only natural that I cross the line from time to time.

This cartoon was killed because the editors felt it was too volatile for the patriotic post 9-11 environment. It was scheduled to run on September 16, 2002.

ABOVE: The 1993 case of pedophile priest James Porter was an early bellwether of a broader scandal that would hit a decade later. My editor at the time was in a no-pedophile-priest-cartoons kind of mood.

BELOW: I was so outraged by the Catholic Church's cover-up in Boston, that I equated it to terrorism. This idea never made it past the sketch stage.

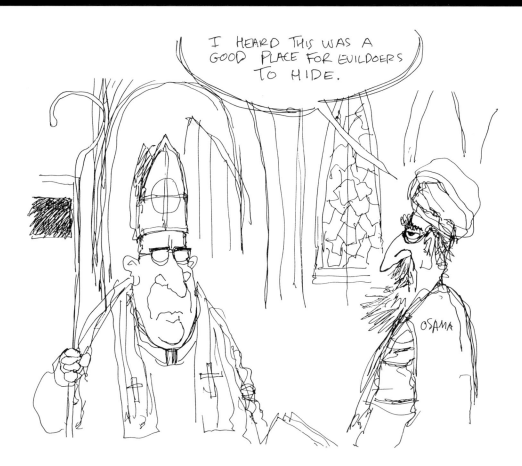

Sometimes I am just out of my mind. Nobody wants to see George W. Bush preparing to milk an old woman. It's wrong on so many levels. This cartoon was drawn after a White House Correspondents dinner where Laura Bush joked that George had "learned a lot about ranching since that first year when he tried to milk the horse."

And finally, cartoons featuring horse feces are an acquired taste. My first editor at *The Pittsburgh Press* loved the cartoon I drew of Reagan riding off into the sunset on a horse, leaving behind a giant pile of horse manure labeled "deficit" for Bush (41) to clean up. But, in 2005, when I drew a cartoon of Michael Brown, who Bush appointed FEMA director even though Brown's previous job was working with Arabian horses, my editor was not as happy with the result. His response to the sketch was, "you're joking, right?"

23

**IS IT OK
TO LAUGH?**

IS IT OK TO LAUGH?

POST 9/11 INK

In the immediate aftermath of 9/11 it wasn't OK to laugh. Letterman and Leno stayed off the air. *Saturday Night Live* waited. Even the gallows office humor that usually follows such events was noticeably absent. It was a time to mourn, reflect and heal. It was also a time to draw. But what does one say about the most horrific tragedy to take place on U.S. soil? How do you draw that?

In the summer of 2001 political cartoonists were concerned with Gary Condit, tax cuts and sharks attacks. Then came September 11th. Suddenly, none of that mattered. Suddenly, nothing was funny. In the days, weeks and even months following the attacks, as the country struggled with feelings of devastating grief, extreme outrage and uplifting patriotism, I attempted to turn those feelings into images. The first images I produced were somber illustrations portraying the tragic yet heroic nature of the event. As time passed and the country began to heal, the cartoons changed as well. A major concern for me has always been how to reconcile a strong national security with the protection of our civil liberties. This chapter includes everything from airport security to bad intelligence to the hunt for Osama bin Laden. Creating these cartoons was part of the healing process for me.

Yes, it's OK to laugh.

Poor airport security is nothing new. I drew this cartoon after a series of hijackings in the eighties. *Published 11/26/85.*

ABOVE LEFT: Unfortunately, hijackings were a problem long before 9/11. They don't have instructions on how to deal with terrorists in the seat pocket in front of you. *Published 01/04/85.*

ABOVE RIGHT: The World Trade Center was a terrorist target in 1993. *Published 08/29/93.*

MIDDLE LEFT: Oklahoma City was the site of some home-grown terrorism. *Published 04/23/95.*

MIDDLE RIGHT: At first, though, we jumped to the wrong conclusion, linking it to the Middle East. *Published 04/25/95.*

LEFT: On September 11, 2001, the country was torn apart by the attacks. *Published 09/13/01.*

ABOVE LEFT: Failed U.S. intelligence was to blame. *Published 09/18/01.*

ABOVE RIGHT: Along with poor airport securtity. *Published 09/20/01.*

MIDDLE LEFT: We began to piece together what happened. *Published 09/25/01.*

MIDDLE RIGHT: Meanwhile, Arab-Americans suffered. *Published 10/06/01.*

LEFT: The Taliban's connection to al-Qaida made them a target for U.S. bombs. *Published 10/07/01.*

ABOVE LEFT: The anthrax scare followed close on the heels of 9/11, sending people running for the antibiotic Cipro. *Published 10/18/01.*

ABOVE RIGHT: The people of Afghanistan were also in a panic. *Published 10/20/01.*

MIDDLE LEFT: Advertisers were capitalizing on the patriotic fervor. *Published 10/25/01.*

MIDDLE RIGHT: The first step in the new Department of Homeland Security's plan was to convince everyone to be very afraid. *Published 11/01/01.*

LEFT: There were plans to bail out the businesses hurt by 9/11. *Published 11/06/01.*

Meanwhile, Liberty was getting frisked. *Published 10/11/01.*

CORPORATE AMERICA DOES ITS PART FOR THE WAR EFFORT...

ABOVE LEFT: Bush kept smoking adjectives out of their holes. *Published 11/08/01.*

ABOVE RIGHT: Corporate America patriotically saved their bottom line. *Published 11/10/01.*

MIDDLE LEFT: Attorney General John Ashcroft quoted this cartoon word for word at the Senate Judiciary Committee hearings on how new anti-terrorism tactics would affect civil liberties. One Senator replied, "I am not sure everybody in America is laughing at that." *Published 11/27/01.*

MIDDLE RIGHT: The holiday season was hard to get excited about. *Published 01/03/02.*

LEFT: The firm of Arthur Andersen was convicted of obstruction of justice for shredding documents related to its audit of Enron. *Published 01/17/02.*

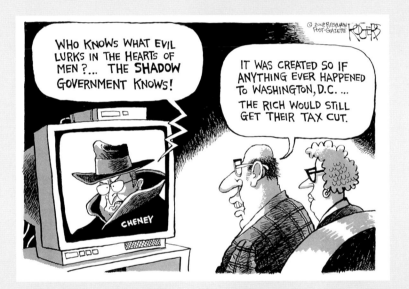

ABOVE LEFT: The Bush/Cheney White House refused to turn over documents revealing what industry pals attended meetings to create U.S. Energy Policy. *Published 02/19/02.*

ABOVE RIGHT: The Pentagon decided they could trip up terrorists by feeding false stories to the media. The plan was dropped after everyone told them how idiotic it was. *Published 02/24/02.*

MIDDLE LEFT: It was revealed that on September 11th, Cheney was whisked away to an undisclosed location to form an emergency "shadow government." *Published 03/05/02.*

MIDDLE RIGHT: Six months after the terrorist attacks, the INS approved student visas for two of the 9/11 hijackers. *Published 03/17/02.*

LEFT: It was also discovered that an FBI memo warning that supporters of Osama bin Laden were attending U.S. flight schools was written in July of 2001. The memo never made it up the chain of command. *Published 05/19/02.*

ABOVE LEFT: John Ashcroft spent $8,000 to cover partially nude statues in the Justice Department because he didn't like being photographed in front of them. *Published 06/06/02.*

ABOVE RIGHT: Bush continued to talk tough on terrorism, even when promoting his fitness initiative. *Published 06/22/02.*

BELOW: On the first anniversary of September 11th the nation was still hurting, but it was clear Bush had already moved on. *Published 09/17/02.*

24

**THE EARS
HAVE IT**

THE EARS HAVE IT

HOW TO DRAW GEORGE W. BUSH
WITHOUT ENDING UP IN GUANTANAMO

George W. Bush was a cartoonist's dream. He had the swagger of John Wayne, the ego of Donald Trump and the conscience of Alfred E. Newman. And what was with that smirk? It seemed to show up at the most inappropriate times like when he was talking about dead soldiers or tsunami victims. And, of course, there were those fabulous ears. In 1999, before I really knew much about Dubya, I drew his ears a normal size. Then, as his policies and attitude became more absurd, so did his ears. It's odd that someone with such big ears, even if they were cartoon ears, could be so deaf to the concerns of average Americans. How did I manage to draw George W. Bush without ending up in Gitmo? I don't really know.

As you can see, I didn't always draw him as Dumbo.

THE EVOLUTION OF THE EARS

July 1999---------November 1999-----May 2000-------January 2001-----September 2004

My sketchbook is the place where my ideas either come to life or go to die. I start by writing down a list of potential topics pulled from that day's headlines. Then, with plenty of coffee to jump-start my brain, I stare at the list until one or two topics jump out at me. Next, I stare out into space until an idea comes to me (I know, a lot of staring is required in this job.) Then, I rough out ideas in my sketchbook. If the idea works as a simple pen and ink sketch, I pencil it in on Bristol board and then finish it off using brush and ink.

The next 3 pages show some examples of my sketchbook drawings. Brace yourself.

ON THE SECOND ANNIVERSARY OF KATRINA, CONDITIONS IN NEW ORLEANS WERE STILL BAD.

AT THE SAME TIME, VIOLENCE IN AFGHANISTAN WAS ESCALATING AND LARRY CRAIG WAS MAKING HEADLINES.

LIST OF POSSIBLE TOPICS

THIS SKETCH ENDED UP AS A CARTOON OF A "FAMILY VALUES" ELEPHANT STEPPING ON UNCLE SAM'S FOOT IN A BATHROOM STALL

THE ORIGINAL SKETCH...

...AND THE FINISHED CARTOON

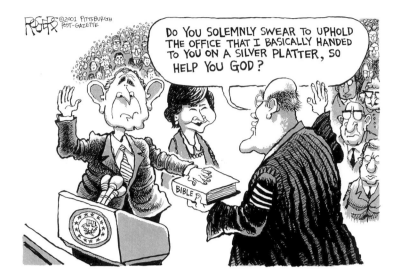

ABOVE LEFT: Dubya managed to make his presidency controversial before he even took the oath of office. *Published 01/20/01.*

ABOVE RIGHT: He made it clear very early that he was a man of faith. *Published 02/01/01.*

MIDDLE LEFT: For instance, he had a lot of faith in tax cuts for the rich. *Published 02/06/01.*

MIDDLE RIGHT: The threat of Reagan-era deficits didn't scare him at all. *Published 03/06/01.*

LEFT: When Cheney's heart problems arose, many worried about the man who was a heartbeat away. *Published 03/08/01.*

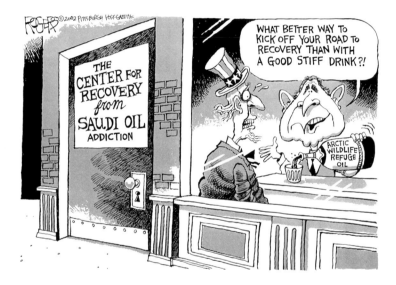

ABOVE LEFT: Cheney was only one of the things Dubya borrowed from the eighties. *Published 03/25/01.*

ABOVE RIGHT: Another eighties holdover, "Star Wars" missile defense, fascinated the younger Bush. Published *05/06/01.*

MIDDLE LEFT: Bush's answer to the country's unhealthy addiction to oil was to find more oil. *Published 03/19/02.*

MIDDLE RIGHT: In 2002, Dubya choked on a pretzel. *Published 01/15/02.*

LEFT: "Homeland Security" became a popular phrase following September 11th. *Published 01/29/02.*

Bush began talking about retooling Social Security. Around the same time, Hollywood came out with a remake of *Planet of the Apes*. *Published 07/29/01.*

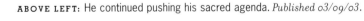

ABOVE LEFT: He continued pushing his sacred agenda. *Published 03/09/03.*

ABOVE RIGHT: With the help of Congress, his proposed tax cuts became a reality. *Published 06/01/03.*

MIDDLE LEFT: The West Nile Virus scare made 2003 a bad year for mosquitoes. *Published 06/29/03.*

MIDDLE RIGHT: Bush was criticized for making a false claim that Iraq tried to obtain uranium in Africa. At first, the CIA was blamed. Later, Bush tried to take responsibility for his words. This "bad intelligence" was the basis for his invasion of Iraq. *Published 07/31/03.*

BELOW LEFT: On May 1, 2003, President Bush landed on an aircraft carrier and officially declared the end to major combat in Iraq. Someone decided it would be a good idea to commemorate this event with a Bush action figure. *Published 08/23/03.*

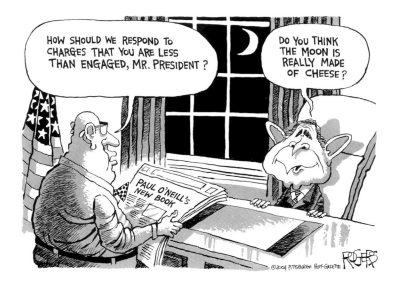

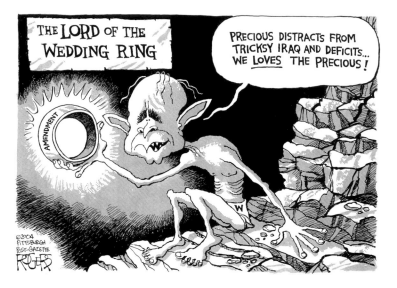

ABOVE LEFT: When the White House leaked the identity of CIA agent, Valerie Plame, Dubya decided he could handle the investigation himself. *Published 10/05/03.*

ABOVE RIGHT: Freedom was important, but not more important than trade. *Published 12/13/03.*

MIDDLE LEFT: Former Treasury Secretary, Paul O'Neill, painted an unflattering portrait of President Bush in his book. *Published 01/15/04.*

MIDDLE RIGHT: Peter Jackson's Oscar-winning *Lord of the Rings* films revealed Gollum to be a perfect metaphor for Bush's infatuation with heterosexual marriage. *Published 03/02/04.*

LEFT: Bush had trouble identifying the real culprits. *Published 02/10/05.*

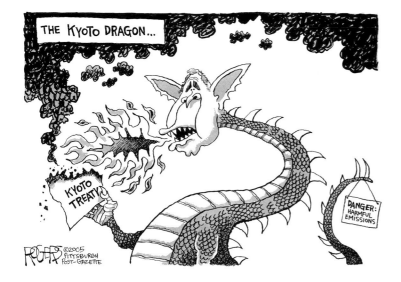

ABOVE LEFT: Bush took care of business by limiting class-action suits. *Published 02/20/05.*

ABOVE RIGHT: Jeff Gannon, a conservative "pro-family" member of the White House press corps, was exposed for using a fake name, having no journalism credentials and posing for gay porn sites. So much for security. At the same time, the White House was paying conservative pundits to sell their policies. *Published 02/22/05.*

MIDDLE LEFT: Global warming was nothing more than a myth to George W. *Published 02/27/05.*

MIDDLE RIGHT: Despite his height, Bush began to appear smaller in my cartoons. I liked to call him the "pocket president." *Published 06/21/05.*

LEFT: Justice Sandra Day O'Connor announced her retirement. *Published 07/07/05.*

ABOVE: The investigation into the White House leak continued. *Published 07/14/05.*

BELOW: Dubya came out in favor of Intelligent Design. *Published 08/06/05.*

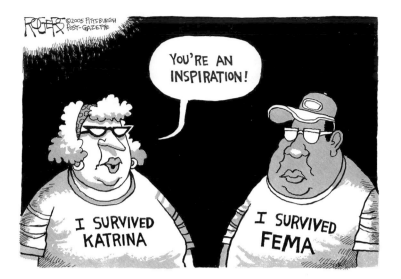

ABOVE LEFT: FEMA failed to do its job after Hurricane Katrina devastated New Orleans. *Published 09/10/05.*

ABOVE RIGHT: Accusations of racism persisted. *Published 09/18/05.*

MIDDLE LEFT: The White House reacted quickly to the news of Supreme Court Justice William H. Rehnquist's death. The victims of Katrina were not so lucky. *Published 09/08/05.*

MIDDLE RIGHT: The tide of criticism rose around the President. *Published 09/11/05.*

LEFT: Bush nominated longtime friend and personal lawyer, Harriet Miers, to fill Justice O'Connor's seat. *Published 10/04/05.*

The New York Times apologized for not reining in reporter Judith Miller and her pro-Bush war coverage. *Published 10/27/05.*

ABOVE LEFT: At every turn, the White House continued to operate under a cloak of secrecy. *Published 11/05/05.*

ABOVE RIGHT: When it was discovered that the Bush administration had been spying on targeted Americans without obtaining warrants, critics accused the President of stepping beyond his constitutional authority. *Published 01/12/06.*

MIDDLE LEFT: Vice President Dick Cheney accidentally shot a friend while quail hunting. *Published 02/14/06.*

MIDDLE RIGHT: The man he shot, Harry Whittington, felt strangely compelled to apologize to Cheney. *Published 02/24/06.*

LEFT: Bush took a trip to visit the growing strategic and economic powers in South Asia. *Published 03/08/06.*

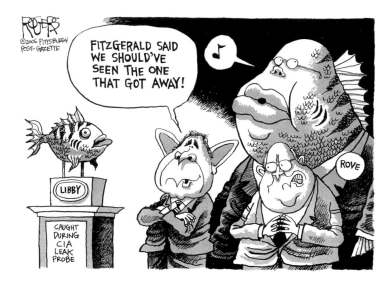

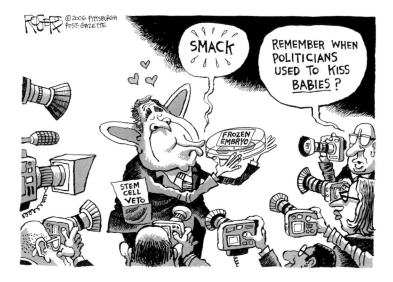

ABOVE LFET: Gas prices were going up as fast as Bush's poll numbers were declining. *Published 04/27/06.*

ABOVE RIGHT: The administration's controversial NSA spying program included collecting phone records of ordinary Americans. *Published 05/12/06.*

MIDDLE LEFT: The FBI gets a tip Jimmy Hoffa might be buried on farm in Michigan. Despite a lot of digging, they find nothing. *Published 05/21/06.*

MIDDLE RIGHT: Special prosecutor Patrick J. Fitzgerald, indicted Dick Cheney's chief of staff, "Scooter" Libby, for leaking the name of CIA agent Valerie Plame. Karl Rove, who also leaked her identity, was left untouched. *Published 06/20/06.*

MIDDLE RIGHT: Bush used his veto power to crush stem cell research. *Published 08/17/06.*

ABOVE LEFT: A provocative title helped generate cult-like Internet buzz for a horror movie starring Samuel L. Jackson. I could just imagine how the President would've reviewed the film. *Published 07/21/06.*

ABOVE RIGHT: Even though a year had passed since Katrina, there was still a lot of rebuilding to do. *Published 08/29/06.*

MIDDLE LEFT: Tom Cruise and Katie Holmes finally released photos of their baby to *Vanity Fair* Magazine. They weren't the only ones to reveal a secret that week. *Published 09/08/06.*

MIDDLE RIGHT: The White House lied about having ties to convicted lobbyist Jack Abramoff. *Published 10/10/06.*

LEFT: In 2007, Queen Elizabeth came to Washington to meet our royal family. *Published 05/10/07.*

ABOVE LEFT: Bush ignored patients who might have benefited from stem cell research. *Published 06/21/07.*

ABOVE RIGHT: Dick Cheney refused to turn over secret documents, claiming that he wasn't beholden to any branch of government. At the same time, the Bald Eagle was taken off the endangered species list. *Published 07/01/07.*

MIDDLE LEFT: Loyal Bushies were leaving the administration in droves, often under clouds of suspicion. *Published 08/30/07.*

MIDDLE RIGHT: Bush vetoed a bill to help uninsured kids. He was against coddling, unless it involved wealthy corporations. *Published 10/04/07.*

LEFT: Nearly all of his sacred mantras had to be amended. *Published 12/06/07.*

ABOVE: His failed presidency was the talk of the town. *Published 02/24/08.*

BELOW: Bush met with Pope Benedict when he came to Washington. *Published 04/17/08.*

ABOVE LEFT: The rebuilt levee in New Orleans held up after another big storm. That's more than I can say about the crumbling Bush Legacy. *Published 06/22/08.*

ABOVE RIGHT: The Bush Justice Department couldn't hide its partisanship, even under those black robes. *Published 07/13/08.*

MIDDLE LEFT: Not even Sarah Palin could erase Bush's troubles. *Published 09/19/08.*

MIDDLE RIGHT: Dubya tried to look presidential during an economic meltdown. *Published 09/30/08.*

LEFT: Oliver Stone's movie about the 43rd president was released in October, three months before the star left office. *Published 10/23/08.*

If only we could regift a president! *Published 12/26/08.*

SELLING THE WAR

You know the uncomfortable feeling you get when a pushy
salesman is trying to sell you something you don't need?
That's how I felt hearing Bush talk about the war in Iraq.
Part of me was embarrassed for him because he looked foolish
trying so hard to pitch a defective product. The other part of
me was angry because he was wasting America's time with lies
and doubletalk. In the end we've all been stuck paying for
something we don't want or need. That doesn't even take into
account the valuable lives lost. If only he had been selling
vacuum cleaners.

Preoccupation with Saddam Hussein is a Bush family legacy. *Published 02/20/01.*

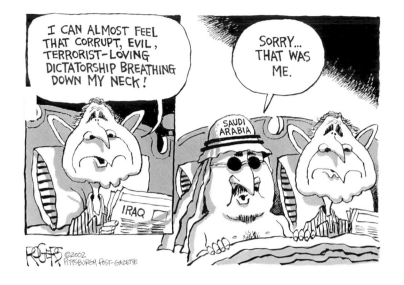

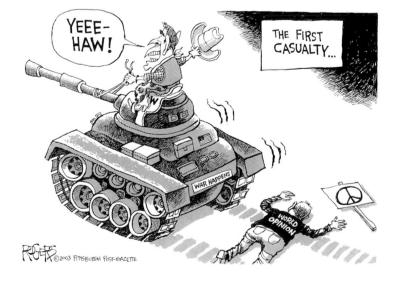

ABOVE LEFT: Another family legacy is their love for the terrorist-producing, oil-producing Saudis. *Published 08/31/02.*

ABOVE RIGHT: A "coalition of the willing" never really materialized. *Published 01/25/03.*

MIDDLE LEFT: Bush kept pushing the unproven connection between Saddam and 9/11. *Published 02/16/03.*

MIDDLE RIGHT: He even took his pitch to the American people. *Published 03/01/03.*

LEFT: The war was on! *Published 03/20/03.*

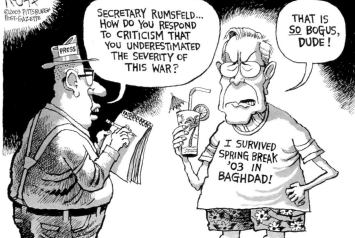

ABOVE LEFT: Dubya promised we'd be greeted as liberators. *Published 03/22/03.*

ABOVE RIGHT: The financial cost of the war began mounting. *Published 03/23/03.*

MIDDLE LEFT: The Pentagon underestimated the amount of troops that would be needed. *Published 04/06/03.*

MIDDLE RIGHT: Saddam's statue came down with the usual American flare. *Published 04/10/03.*

LEFT: Some felt handing out tax cuts during wartime was irresponsible. Bush didn't agree. *Published 04/12/03.*

ABOVE LEFT: Our image abroad fell like Saddam's regime. *Published 04/20/03.*

ABOVE RIGHT: Religious extremists made life difficult for average Iraqis. *Published 05/01/03.*

BELOW: Freedom … er, I mean, Halliburton was on the march. *Published 04/27/03.*

ABOVE LEFT: Bush continued asking for outside support. *Published 09/25/03.*

ABOVE RIGHT: The economy wasn't joining the coalition either. *Published 05/06/03.*

MIDDLE LEFT: Oops! No WMDs were ever found. *Published 10/07/03.*

MIDDLE RIGHT: Saddam's hiding place, on the other hand, was found. *Published 12/18/03.*

LEFT: Despite the evidence, Bush couldn't let go of the imaginary WMDs. *Published 01/31/04.*

ABOVE: Torture photos from Abu Ghraib prison didn't help the war effort. *Published 05/09/04.*

BELOW: The new Iraqi interim government became a target. *Published 06/20/04.*

ABOVE LEFT: Bush continued to insist things were going well. *Published 10/12/04.*

ABOVE RIGHT: Iraqi women were feeling exposed. *Published 08/18/05.*

MIDDLE LEFT: The imprisoned Saddam suffered an unflattering photo-op in his underwear. *Published 05/24/05.*

MIDDLE RIGHT: Two years after Dubya declared "mission accomplished," things were looking less and less accomplished. *Published 05/08/05.*

LEFT: He continued to justify the sacrifice in Iraq by invoking September 11th. *Published 08/23/05.*

Rumsfeld responded inadequately to complaints of inadequate body armor. *Published 12/12/04.*

ABOVE LEFT: Bush complained that the media was only reporting negative news from Iraq. *Published 03/26/06.*

ABOVE RIGHT: Unlike Iraq, Bush showed surprising restraint when it came to Iran's weapons of mass destruction. At the same time, scientists discovered the fossils of a 375-million-year-old fish, the missing link in the evolution from water to land. *Published 04/13/06.*

MIDDLE LEFT: The President gloated when al-Qaida terrorist, Abu Musab al-Zarqawi, was killed. *Published 06/09/06.*

MIDDLE RIGHT: The White House was quick to criticize John Kerry for a botched joke about how poor grades could land someone in Iraq. He was joking about Bush, not the military. *Published 11/05/06.*

LEFT: In the 2006 midterm election, anti-war voters gave the Republicans a serious "timeout." *Published 11/09/06.*

ABOVE LEFT: James Baker was brought in to help fix Iraq. *Published 11/28/06.*

ABOVE RIGHT: The number of Americans killed in Iraq surpassed the number killed on September 11th. *Published 12/28/06.*

MIDDLE LEFT: Bush continued to disregard Congress when it came to the war. *Published 02/15/07.*

MIDDLE RIGHT: He blamed the Democrats for deserting the troops. *Published 04/03/07.*

LEFT: Tony Blair's career ended on a sour note after unabashedly supporting Bush and the war in Iraq. *Published 05/11/07.*

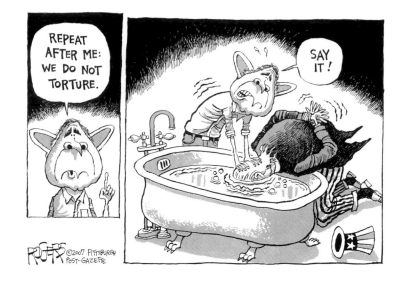

ABOVE LEFT: Six years after 9/11 there was still no sign of bin Laden. *Published 09/09/07.*

ABOVE RIGHT: The White House continued to deny that what they were doing constituted torture. *Published 10/07/07.*

MIDDLE LEFT: While California was battling a deadly wildfire, Bush was threatening Iran. *Published 11/02/07.*

MIDDLE RIGHT: Bush tried to stimulate the economy with rebate checks. *Published 05/01/08.*

LEFT: We all have to sacrifice in times of war. Bush gave up golf. *Published 05/20/08.*

Osama bin Laden's driver was convicted by a military tribunal. *Published 08/10/08.*

On his final visit to Iraq, Bush was greeted with footwear. *Published 12/16/08.*

25 NO CARTOON LEFT BEHIND!

NO CARTOON LEFT BEHIND!

ACTUALLY, I HAVE MORE IN THE BASEMENT

One of the problems with putting together a book like this is that life doesn't always fit neatly into categories. Neither does the news. Occasionally my job calls for something outside the rectangle on the editorial page. In 1994 I had a cartoon on the cover of *Newsweek*. In 1996 I traveled to Moscow and covered the Russian election. This chapter is just what it sounds like: odds and ends that didn't fit neatly in any other chapter. It also serves as an overflow for cartoons I accidentally overlooked or drew after finishing a chapter.

Enjoy!

Welfare reform became a popular theme in the '96 election. *Published 07/23/96.*

REPRINTS

A "reprint" is the publication of a cartoon in a major magazine
or newspaper after it first appears in the cartoonist's home
paper. My first reprint came just six months after embarking
on my career. It appeared in the October 1, 1984 issue of *Time*.
I was floored! I thought this was the beginning of endless
reprints, fame and fortune. I was wrong. I wouldn't get another
reprint until the summer of 1985. Eventually, after three years
of diligently sending out my cartoons to assorted publications,
it began to pay off. By 1988 I had snagged enough reprints to
catch the attention of *United Feature Syndicate*, who sent me
a contract. They actually wanted to distribute my cartoons!
I thought this was the beginning of endless reprints, fame and
fortune. I was wrong again. But it hasn't taken away the thrill
of seeing my work reprinted in major publications. Every time
I see one it feels like October 1984.

ABOVE LEFT: My first reprinted cartoon depicted Soviet Foreign Minister
Andrei Gromyko's visit to the U.S. during the 1984 presidential campaign.

ABOVE RIGHT: My cartoon appeared on the same page with cartoons by well-
known editorial cartoonists Jack Ohman and Jeff MacNelley. Years later, Jack
told me he remembers seeing the page and wondering, "who the hell is this guy?"

ABOVE: Mondale wasn't about to let Reagan steal the entire campaign spotlight in 1984. Well, not until November, that is.

BELOW: My second major reprint appeared in the *Washington Post* in 1985. During the mid-eighties the world witnessed a rash of hijackings and other terrorist activities.

ABOVE: My third major reprint appeared in *The New York Times* later that year. That was the year Springsteen's "Born in the U.S.A." was released. It was also a time when Reagan and Congress were sparring over foreign trade.

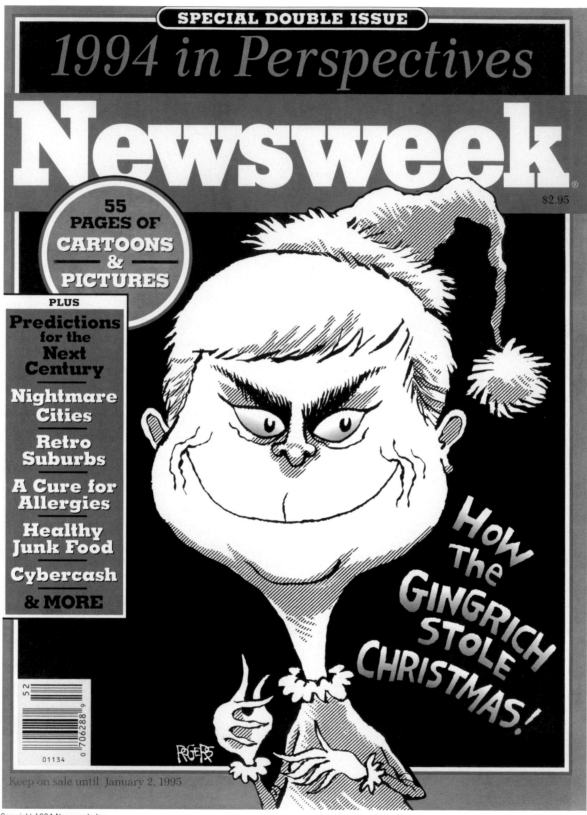

ABOVE: Former Speaker of the House, Newt Gingrich, helped orchestrate the GOP takeover of Congress in 1994. I drew him as the "Gingrich Who Stole Christmas" for *Newsweek's* year-end issue.

PERSPECTIVES

"It's all true. We are space aliens. I'm amazed that it's taken you so long to find out."

SEN. PHIL GRAMM *of Texas, reacting to a supermarket-tabloid story headlined* 12 SENATORS ARE FROM OUTER SPACE!

■ "I begged them to send troops . . . Unfortunately, let us say with great humility, I failed. It is a scandal. I am the first one to say it." *United Nations Secretary-General* BOUTROS BOUTROS-GHALI, *admitting the failure of U.N. efforts to halt the Rwanda slaughter*

■ "I hate to say this, but I believe my children will be safer in Bujumbura than in Washington, D.C." *Former senator* BOB KRUEGER, *on his new ambassadorial appointment to the capital of Burundi, the nation next door to Rwanda*

■ "Now if only someone would ask us somewhere smart." QUEEN ELIZABETH II, *in a remark reportedly made as she eyed herself in a new outfit by royal dressmaker Sir Hardy Amies*

■ "You are the biggest hypocrite in the room . . . What you have done is turn your life into a total lie. You talk about the Koran. You have shamed it . . . You violated the laws not only of man but of God." *U.S. Judge* KEVIN DUFFY, *to one of four men convicted in the World Trade Center bombing, who suggested they acted out God's will. Duffy sentenced each to 240 years.*

■ "We cannot solve every such outburst of civil strife or militant nationalism simply by sending in our forces." BILL CLINTON, *on the conflict in Rwanda, which has so far claimed more than 200,000 lives*

■ "I really can't pronounce his name, but it is something like 'Cheese Nachos'." *How a C-Span caller recently tried to identify HUD Secretary Henry Cisneros, as related by the Latino cabinet secretary himself*

■ " . . . When we were . . . waiting for President and Mrs. Clinton to arrive, Jackie turned to me and said, 'Teddy, you go down and greet the president.' But I said, 'Maurice [Tempelsman] is already there.' And Jackie answered, 'Teddy, you do it. Maurice isn't running for re-election.' She was always there—for all our family—in her special way." *Sen.* EDWARD M. KENNEDY, *in his eulogy at the funeral mass for Jacqueline Kennedy Onassis in New York City*

ABOVE: In 1995 the wise folks at *Newsweek* chose my cartoons for all three slots on their Perspectives page. As far as I know, this was a first for the magazine. The only hitch was that they erroneously credited my third cartoon to Frank Cammuso of Syracuse.

ABOVE, BELOW AND OPPOSITE: My newspaper sent me to Moscow the week before the 1996 Russian election. Boris Yeltsin was struggling to maintain power amid a "re-birth" of the communist party.

This ten panel cartoon was drawn for the 1997 Year-In-Review issue of *Newsweek*.

In case you can't recall all of the news of 1997, here are a few clues:

1: Saddam Hussein continued to taunt the world by expelling the U.N. weapons inspectors. 2: British au pair Louise Woodward was found guilty of second-degree murder after shaking the baby she was caring for. The charge was later reduced to manslaughter. 3: Marv Albert was accused of sexually assaulting a woman and biting her on the back. 4: Mike Tyson was disqualified in a rematch with Evander Holyfield for biting both of his ears. 5: Members of Heaven's Gate, an American UFO religion led by Marshall Applewhite, committed mass suicide. All 39 of them were wearing identical black shirts, sweat pants and brand new black-and-white Nike athletic shoes. 6: Frank Gifford was video-taped having an affair with a former stewardess. At the same time, Kelly Flinn, the first female B-52 pilot in the United States Air Force, faced a court-martial for charges of adultery. The media circus embarrassed the Air Force and she was later allowed to resign. 7: Ellen DeGeneres, whose show was doing poorly, decided it was a good time to "come out." 8: Paula Jones filed a civil lawsuit against sitting president, Bill Clinton. 9: Al Gore was criticized for making fundraising calls from his White House office. 10: After Princess Diana's death, paparazzi were vilified more than ever.

RANDOM LEFTOVERS

This section serves as an overflow for cartoons that were either overlooked the first time around, didn't fit neatly into the flow of a particular chapter or were drawn recently and added at the last minute. For instance, some of my favorite cartoons are about computers and the Internet, but, unfortunately, they seem to have fallen through the cracks. I am including them here.

Putting this book together made me feel a little like Steve Martin's character in *The Jerk* when he is leaving his mansion saying, "I don't need this or this. Just this ashtray. And this paddle game, the ashtray and the paddle game and that's all I need. And this remote control ...." He continues to update the list of things he "needs" on his way out. While working on this book, I found myself looking back at cartoons I had just drawn that day or week and updating my list of ones I "needed" in the book.

THE 1980s

ABOVE: In 1984, surgeons attempted to transplant a baboon heart into a human. *Published 11/01/84.*

BELOW: The Christmas decorations seem to come out sooner and sooner every year. I wonder how the original pilgrims handled this. *Published 11/26/84.*

ABOVE LEFT: Unisex insurance became more common around the time Boy George was popular. *Published 12/11/84.*

ABOVE RIGHT: Pittsburgh winters can be pretty cold. Every year I hear lots of weather complaints referencing witches and well diggers. *Published 01/22/85.*

MIDDLE LEFT: The Gramm-Rudman measure was designed to automatically cut the budget if Congress failed to do the necessary work to reduce it. *Published 12/15/85.*

MIDDLE RIGHT: Around the same time, Sylvester Stallone was keeping busy with his *Rambo* movies. *Published 01/17/86.*

BELOW LEFT: A shadow was cast over NASA's shuttle program when the *Challenger* exploded shortly after takeoff. *Published 01/29/86.*

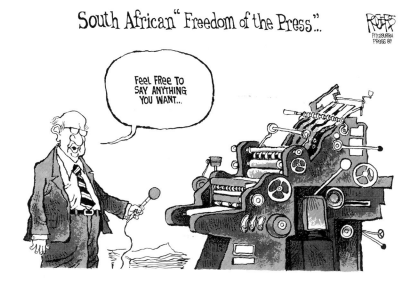

South African "Freedom of the Press"...

ABOVE LEFT: NASA found it difficult to piece together exactly what happened. *Published 02/21/86.*

ABOVE RIGHT: In 1986 the Statue of Liberty celebrated its 200th birthday in style. *Published 07/03/86.*

MIDDLE LEFT: The art world was shocked to discover Andrew Wyeth had been secretly drawing and painting his neighbor, Helga, for fifteen years. *Published 08/12/86.*

MIDDLE RIGHT: Apartheid in South Africa began to get people's attention. *Published 08/11/87.*

BELOW LEFT: True freedom of the press was still elusive in South Africa. *Published 01/11/87.*

ABOVE: College tuition and health care costs were both on the rise. *Published 02/11/87.*

BELOW: In 1987, Attorney General Ed Meese came under scrutiny for his role in the Iran-Contra scandal. He couldn't recall seeing anything. *Published 07/02/87.*

THREE BLIND MEESE

OLYMPIC GOLD

ABOVE: The 1988 Olympics were disrupted when sprinter Ben Johnson was stripped of his gold medal after failing the drug test. *Published 09/22/88.*

BELOW LEFT: Steroid use was a hot topic long before Barry Bonds came along. *Published 12/18/88.*

BELOW RIGHT: I thought this cartoon summed up the hazards of the eighties pretty well. *Published 01/01/89.*

THE 1990s

ABOVE RIGHT: Nelson Mandela's wife, Winnie, was jailed in South Africa. On the bright side, no one had to make new protest signs. *Published 05/16/91.*

MIDDLE LEFT: The Pittsburgh Penguins won the Stanley Cup, finally joining the Pirates and Steelers as national champs. *Published 06/18/91.*

MIDDLE RIGHT: Elvis got a stamp. *Published 01/17/92.*

BELOW LEFT: Medical testing begins at home. *Published 03/06/93.*

BELOW RIGHT: In the midst of dealing with the Paula Jones scandal, Bill Clinton finds out he has a long-lost half brother. *Published 06/22/93.*

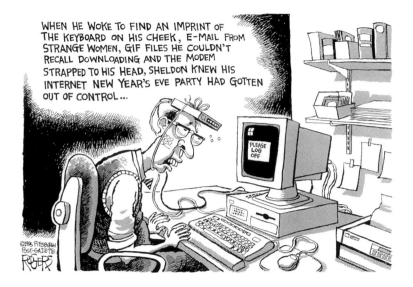

ABOVE LEFT: Software companies are like drug dealers who keep their users coming back for a never-ending supply of upgrades. *Published 08/24/95.*

ABOVE RIGHT: The Internet quickly grew into a place to socialize. Some hard-core geeks even rang in the New Year online. *Published 12/31/95.*

MIDDLE LEFT: After the disastrous results in Waco and Ruby Ridge, the FBI changed their stakeout techniques. *Published 03/31/96.*

MIDDLE RIGHT: The courts limited the amounts awarded in punitive damage cases. *Published 05/26/96.*

BELOW LEFT: Welfare reform became a popular theme in the '96 election. *Published 07/23/96.*

ABOVE LEFT: Pot smoking became an issue in politics when ex-hippies started running for office. *Published 12/05/96.*

MIDDLE LEFT: Gingrich was accused of hypocrisy and unethical behavior when he accepted a $4.5 million advance as part of a book deal. *Published 01/23/97.*

MIDDLE RIGHT: Bill Clinton underwent knee surgery. Meanwhile, Attorney General Janet Reno refused to bow to GOP pressure to seek the appointment of an independent counsel to investigate fundraising abuses in Clinton's 1996 presidential campaign. *Published 03/18/97.*

BELOW LEFT: The Supreme Court ruled in favor of protecting Internet porn as free speech. The same kind of free speech Justice Thomas used when inappropriately discussing porn films with Anita Hill. *Published 07/05/97.*

BELOW RIGHT: Mac and Microsoft decided to try to work together. *Published 08/10/97.*

ABOVE: Sweepstakes companies agreed to be more honest with their letters. *Published 03/19/98.*

BELOW: In 1998, over 100 million were said to be using the internet. *Published 04/18/98.*

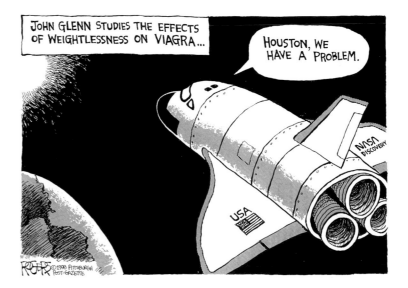

ABOVE LEFT: Corporate mergers became all the rage in the late '90s. *Published 04/19/98.*

ABOVE RIGHT: Al Gore proposed his "plain talk initiative" to help government eliminate bureaucratic paperwork. Imagine all the bureaucratic writers who ended up jobless and on the street. *Published 06/07/98.*

MIDDLE LEFT: The live webcast was born. *Published 06/18/98.*

MIDDLE RIGHT: John Glenn joined a shuttle mission to test the effects of space on the elderly. *Published 10/27/98.*

BELOW LEFT: Bill Gates continued to strangle the competition. *Published 10/29/98.*

ABOVE LEFT: The AOL/Netscape merger challenged Micrsoft's invincibility. *Published 12/28/98.*

ABOVE RIGHT: NASA lost its Mars Orbiter due to a mistake in navigational measurements. One team was using English units while the other team was using the metric system. *Published 10/07/99.*

MIDDLE LEFT: NYC Mayor, Rudolph Giuliani, threatened to withdraw funding from the Brooklyn Museum of Art if they did not pull Chris Ofili's painting, *The Holy Virgin Mary*, which contained elephant dung. *Published 10/09/99.*

MIDDLE RIGHT: Charles Schulz decided to stop drawing his popular comic strip, *Peanuts. Published 12/16/99.*

BELOW LEFT: The night before his final comic strip was published, he passed away. *Published 02/15/00.*

THE 2000s

ABOVE: Hillary Clinton reached out to New York voters during her Senate race, which happened to coincide with an all-New York World Series. *Published 10/24/00.*

MIDDLE RIGHT: The National Zoo in Washington, D.C., put their Panda's mating habits on display. *Published 01/14/01.*

BELOW LEFT: It was hard getting past the feeling that the Republicans had stolen the 2000 election. *Published 04/14/01.*

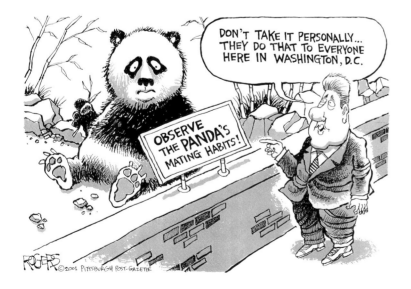

GEORGE HARRISON 1943–2001

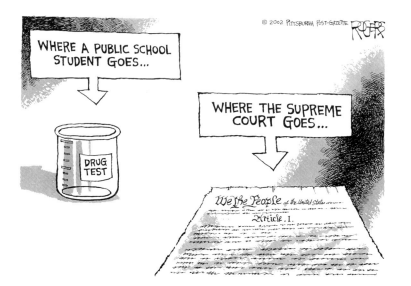

ABOVE LEFT: Bush wanted federal money to go to faith-based organizations. *Published 08/05/01.*

ABOVE RIGHT: The world mourned the loss of another Beatle. *Published 12/04/01.*

MIDDLE LEFT: The Enron hearings got underway around the same time the Boston pedophile priest scandal was making headlines. *Published 03/03/02.*

MIDDLE RIGHT: The Supreme Court ruled that random drug testing in schools was OK. I felt this cartoon was a strong statement in defense of our civil liberties. My editors called it "potty humor" and ended up killing it. *Published 07/06/02.*

BELOW LEFT: Blessed are the poor, unless they look to the U.S. government to help them. *Published 07/07/02.*

ABOVE: A commercial for allergy relief medication made a good metaphor for an insecure world plagued by terror and fear. *Published 04/03/03.*

BELOW: The FDA required that foods containing trans fatty acids be clearly labeled. *Published 07/13/03.*

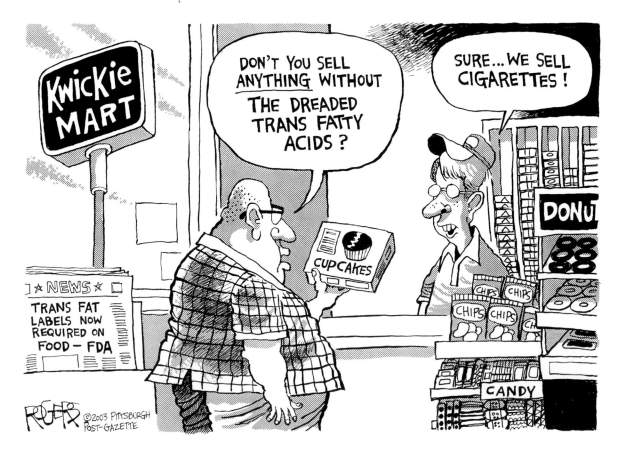

ABOVE: The world was also plagued by spam. *Published 05/03/03.*

BELOW: I hope I live long enough to see a cure for spam. *Published 07/10/03.*

ABOVE LEFT: Arnold Schwarzenegger entered the race for governor against Gray Davis in the California's historic recall election. *Published 06/17/03.*

ABOVE RIGHT: The California race for governor attracted quite a diverse crowd. *Published 08/10/03.*

MIDDLE LEFT: Arnold won the election despite accusations of sexual harassment. *Published 10/04/03.*

MIDDLE RIGHT: The music industry sued kids for illegally downloading music. *Published 09/11/03.*

BELOW: The Patriot Act continued to threaten civil liberties by allowing the government to listen in. *Published 09/27/03.*

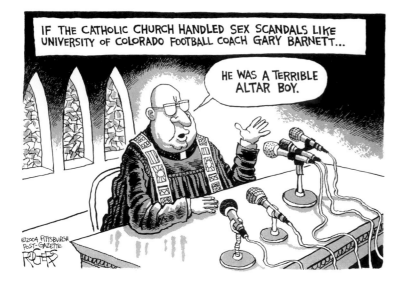

ABOVE LEFT: When a female placekicker at Colorado University accused a teammate of raping her, coach Gary Barnett called her an "awful" player who "couldn't kick the ball through the uprights." He was suspended. *Published 02/29/04.*

ABOVE RIGHT: The Justice Department advised the White House in a 2002 memo that the torture of al-Qaida terror suspects might be legally defensible. The "torture memo" was made public around the same time Bill Clinton's book hit the stands. *Published 06/17/04.*

MIDDLE LEFT: A month after Bill O'Reilly released his *The O'Reilly Factor For Kids*, he was hit with a sexual harassment lawsuit from a former employee who claimed he talked about phone sex, among other things. *Published 10/23/04.*

MIDDLE RIGHT: Despite mounting indictments and a career built on ethics violations, Tom DeLay's friends in the GOP continued to save him from rebuke. After a while, though, even they were getting a bad taste in their mouths. *Published 04/10/05.*

BELOW LEFT: Rick Santorum took pot shots at feminists, liberals and working mothers in his controversial book, *It Takes A Family. Published 07/17/05.*

ABOVE LEFT: Energy costs rose after the Katrina disaster. *Published 10/16/05.*

MIDDLE LEFT: Some cultural rivalries are as old as civilization. *Published 04/09/06.*

MIDDLE RIGHT: Immigration continued to be a contentious issue for average Americans. *Published 05/02/06.*

BELOW LEFT: The U.S. restored full diplomatic relations with Libya, removing them from its list of state sponsors of terrorism. *Published 05/16/06.*

BELOW RIGHT: Americans became obsessed with Brad and Angelina. *Published 06/01/06.*

ABOVE: The GOP's mid-term election campaign revisited their assault on civil liberties. *Published 06/25/06.*

BELOW LEFT: Airports were following suit. *Published 08/18/06.*

BELOW RIGHT: Guantanamo continued to fester. *Published 08/22/06.*

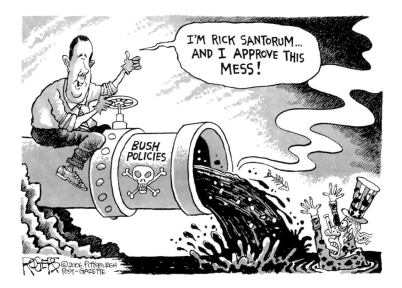

ABOVE LEFT: Speaking of torture, the campaign ads got nastier. *Published 09/28/06.*

ABOVE RIGHT: Congressman Mark Foley was caught sending inappropriate emails to underage pages. The blame game ensued. *Published 10/06/06.*

MIDDLE LEFT: Senator Rick Santorum lost his re-election bid. Many blamed his allegiance to Bush. *Published 10/16/06.*

MIDDLE RIGHT: The Democrats gained control of the House and Senate, only to find out they were both in need of serious repairs. *Published 11/12/06.*

BELOW LEFT: The SUV-heavy auto industry fell on hard times. *Published 01/13/07.*

ABOVE LEFT: Consumers continued to ignore the threat of global warming. *Published 02/06/07.*

ABOVE RIGHT: Astronaut Lisa Nowak made headlines when she drove 900 miles to confront a romantic rival. She wore diapers to limit the need for potty breaks. Meanwhile, Congress showed weak resolve on the war. *Published 02/09/07.*

MIDDLE LEFT: Bush claimed Iran sent arms to Iraq. Naturally, the public was skeptical. *Published 02/20/07.*

MIDDLE RIGHT: A military scandal broke out when deplorable conditions were uncovered at Walter Reed Hospital. *Published 02/27/07.*

BELOW LEFT: The White House accused Democrats of partisan politics when the Democrats accused the White House of partisan politics. *Published 03/22/07.*

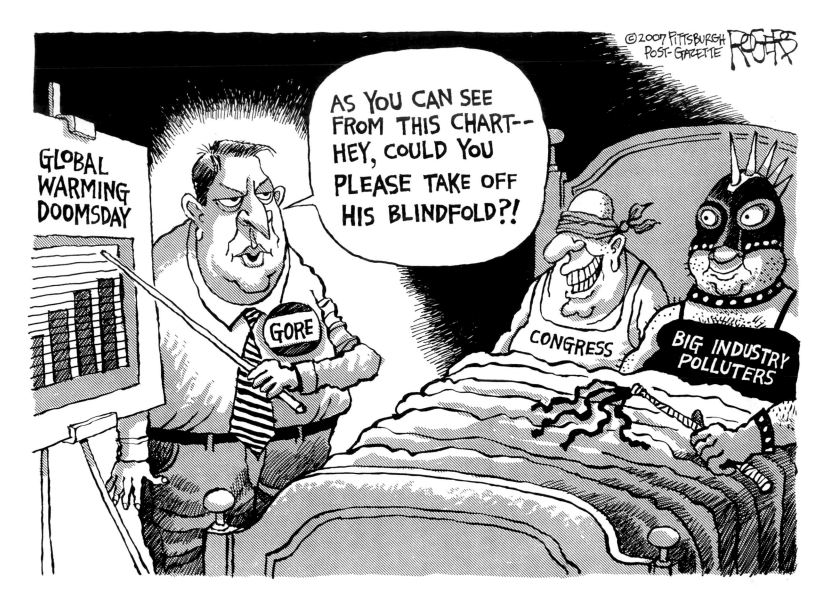

ABOVE: Al Gore took his global warming message to Congress. *Published 03/25/07.*

BELOW LEFT: Lobbyists survived yet another attempt by lawmakers to curb campaign spending. *Published 04/05/07.*

BELOW RIGHT: Don Imus was fired for making racist comments. *Published 04/12/07.*

NBC decided to run
the Virginia Tech
gunman's video rant.
Published 04/22/07.

ABOVE LEFT: Vladimir Putin cracked down on democratic reforms in Russia. *Published 04/29/07.*

ABOVE RIGHT: The infamous D.C. Madam made her client list public. *Published 05/04/07.*

MIDDLE LEFT: Paris Hilton went to jail. *Published 05/13/07.*

MIDDLE RIGHT: Jimmy Carter called George W. Bush the worst president ever. *Published 05/24/07.*

BELOW LEFT: The much-hyped iPhone made its debut. *Published 06/28/07.*

ABOVE LEFT: Secretary of Homeland Security Michael Chertoff claimed he had a "gut feeling" about an increased terror threat. *Published 07/15/07.*

ABOVE RIGHT: Despite their outrage with his handling of the war in Iraq, Republicans on Capitol Hill continued to support President Bush. *Published 07/20/07.*

MIDDLE LEFT: Staunch "family values " senator, Larry Craig, was arrested for soliciting sex in an airport bathroom. *Published 08/31/07.*

MIDDLE RIGHT: Craig denied he was gay. At the same time, Iran president Mahmoud Ahmadinejad denied there were any gays in Iran. *Published 09/27/07.*

BELOW LEFT: The U.S. did little when Myanmar's government cracked down on protesters. *Published 09/30/07.*

ABOVE LEFT: The Patriots lost the Super Bowl to the Giants … and Hillary lost the primary to Obama. *Published 02/05/08.*

MIDDLE LEFT: Despite Obama's popularity, some blacks were still being ignored. *Published 02/12/08.*

MIDDLE RIGHT: Fidel Castro retired. *Published 02/21/08.*

BELOW LEFT: New York Governor Eliot Spitzer resigned in the midst of a prostitution scandal. *Published 03/13/08.*

BELOW RIGHT: Spitzer's wife, like so many wives of politicians, stood by his side while he made his public apology. *Published 03/16/08.*

ABOVE: It was discovered that absurd amounts of pharmaceuticals were winding up in tap water. *Published 03/18/08.*

BELOW: China hosted the 2008 Olympics. They did not medal in human rights. *Published 04/11/08.*

ABOVE: As the polar ice caps continued to melt, even global warming skeptics were having a change of heart. *Published 05/18/08.*

BELOW: It was reported that an alarming number of kids were growing up medicated. *Published 07/10/08.*

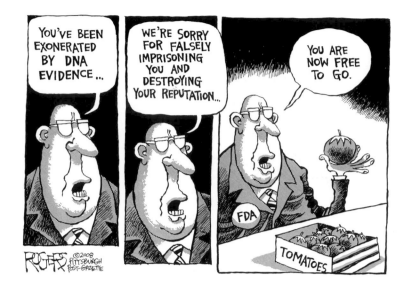

ABOVE LEFT: The FDA wrongly blamed tomatoes for a salmonella outbreak, and later had to retract their claim. *Published 07/24/08.*

ABOVE RIGHT: Hillary was chosen as Obama's Secretary of State but some critics worried that Bill's fundraising might taint the office. At the same time, the Obamas were talking about getting a new White House dog. *Published 11/23/08.*

MIDDLE LEFT: Terrorists attacked the city of Mumbai, India. *Published 12/04/08.*

MIDDLE RIGHT: Rod Blagojevich, Governor of Illinois, was caught in a pay-to-play scheme that included selling Obama's Senate seat. *Published 12/11/08.*

BELOW LEFT: Blagojevich, a gift to cartoonists, was the latest in a long line of corrupt Chicago politicians. *Published 12/18/08.*

ABOVE: The voters were more than eager to see President Obama fix all the country's problems. *Published 01/25/09.*

BELOW: Obama promised to end partisan politics ... but somebody forgot to tell the Republicans. *Published 02/13/09.*

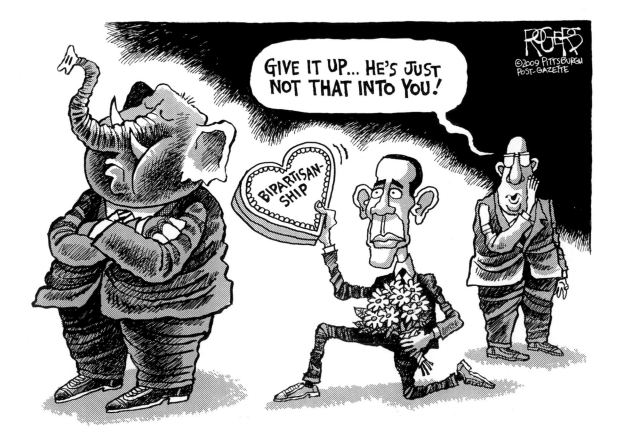

ABOVE LEFT: The new President began the difficult task of undoing some of the deeds of the old President. *Published 03/12/09.*

ABOVE RIGHT: A 2005 memo revealed that the C.I.A., under the Bush administration, used waterboarding 183 times against Khalid Shaikh Mohammed. Apparently, 182 times wasn't enough. *Published 04/24/09.*

BELOW LEFT: As Guantanamo prepared to close, some suggested folding the Gitmo prisoners into the U.S. federal prison system. That made people living near federal prisons very nervous. *Published 05/31/09.*

BELOW RIGHT: President Obama was greeted as a hero when he traveled to the Middle East. *Published 06/05/09.*

ACKNOWLEDGMENTS

Special Thanks (in order of appearance) To:

DAD — for sending me to those museum classes, encouraging me to draw from the start, introducing me to the work of Thurber, Addams, Boothe and many more, buying me that black notebook at age 8 and being OK with my decision to go into art instead of medicine.

MOM (Janet) — for giving birth to me and passing on your artistic genes.

JANET MARIE — for taking on the burden of the first born, helping to raise me, introducing me to track, swimming, hiking and fighting. I'll forgive you for beating me up if you forgive me for the merciless teasing.

LINDA — my beloved sister, for your amazing creativity, bold spirit, uncontional love, support and encouragement over the years. I never would have survived my childhood without you.

MY PHILLY FANMILY — to all of my aunts, uncles, cousins, etc., who helped shape my early years … despite your corrupting influences, I love you all.

MOM (Sandra) — for heroically stepping up and taking on an overwhelming task. I can never find the words to thank you properly for all your love and sacrifice.

BRAD AND **DAVE** — for keeping me humble the way only loving brothers can do … and for making me laugh a lot on Friday nights.

MY OKLAHOMA BUDDIES — especially Joel Dyer, Mike Robbins, Diane Kalousdian, Kevin Meeks and Kevin Moss.

DANNY KETCH — I miss you, buddy. You helped me survive freshman drawing class and your family always made me feel at home. You were taken from us too soon.

HALL DUNCAN — for being an invaluable mentor and encouragement to me. You represent the best of what a teacher can be. (Also, a shout out to your former colleagues at UCO, Dean Hyde and Bill Gallo.)

HERB OLDS — you made drawing a passionate pursuit for me. Your love for the process of making art was contagious. Your gift for teaching was unmatched. (Also, a shout out to your former colleagues at CMU, Harry Holland, Jim Denny and Doug Pickering.)

MY CMU COHORTS — Jamie Adams, Anna Coleman and Gregg Liberi, I miss our days in the Fine Arts building. (Also, a shout out to Gregg Valley, Burton Morris and Jim Quinnan.)

TIM MENEES — for your guidance and friendship, especially when I came to show you my college cartoons. Little did either of us know that your advice would help me land a job at the competing newspaper.

ANGUS McCEACHRAN — for seeing something in an awkward 25-year-old who had never worked for a newspaper and for not giving up on me in the first year when I was I struggling. You will always be a father figure to me. You can decide whether that is good or bad.

ROBERT BIANCO — for the honor of your friendship and the wisdom of your counsel. You helped me hone my political humor. I hope you don't ask for royalties.

MY *PITTSBURGH PRESS* FAMILY — especially John Kaplan, Doug Root, Brian O'Neill, Peter King, Dennis Roddy, Dorothy Conway, Linda Parker, Ed Harrel, Izzy Shrensky, Henry Daubner, Tony Ward and Ralph Brem (with a special shout out to all the great guys in the art department, especially Chuck Livolsi).

JOHN CRAIG — for being the kind of editor who was willing to try new things, including hiring a second editorial cartoonist.

JOHN BLOCK — for being a visionary publisher who still believes in the importance of a local editorial cartoonist to a newspaper's vitality.

TOM WASELESKI — the best editorial page editor a cartoonist could ask for.

THE REST OF MY *POST-GAZETTE* FAMILY — each and every one of you, but especially Mike McGough, Reg Henry, Tony Norman, Alice Rowley, John Allison and the rest of the editorial page.

MY AAEC FAMILY — to the entire balding white-male legion (no offense Etta, Signe and Ann), but especially Scott Stantis, Bruce Plante, Mike Luckovich, Walt Handelsman and Goofus (Joel Pett).

MY TOONSEUNM FAMILY — especially Joe Wos.

MY PITTSBURGH POSSE — especially Steve Mendelson and Matthew Craig.

MOJO — You kept me grounded and sane. I miss our walks together. You ate poop, but you had a heart of gold.

PAUL SCHIFINO — for your patience, friendship and true professionalism in working with me (or should I say putting up with me) over the past five years as we completed this book. Your design work is spectacular.

ALL MY ASSISTANTS — for all your hard work over the years, especially Jared Miller who is helping me type up these acknowledgments.

CMU PRESS — Thanks to Jared Cohon, Jerry Costanzo and Cynthia Lamb for helping to make this book a reality.

ALL MY HEROES — there is not enough room to mention all of the great artists I admire or who influenced me, but here are some of them: The geniuses of *Mad* Magazine (especially Jack Davis), Charles Schulz, Charles Addams, Jay Ward (*Bullwinkle*), George Baker (*Sad Sack*), Jeff MacNelly, Pat Oliphant, Tony Auth, Mike Peters, Herblock, Gary Larson, George Herriman (*Krazy Kat*), E.C. Segar (*Popeye*), Ronald Searle, Al Hirschfeld, David Levine, and Edward Sorel.

And finally, special thanks to:

SYLVIA — for making me a better human being and a better cartoonist. You constantly inspire me. No one makes me think harder or laugh harder. Your love and friendship have meant the world to me.

Rob Rogers is the award-winning editorial cartoonist for the *Pittsburgh Post-Gazette*. His cartoons have been vexing and entertaining readers in Pittsburgh for 25 years. Syndicated by *United Feature Syndicate*, Rogers' work also appears in *The New York Times*, *The Washington Post*, *USA Today* and *Newsweek*, among others.

Rogers is an active member (and past president) of the *Association of American Editorial Cartoonists*. His work received the 2000 *Thomas Nast Award* from the Overseas Press Club and the 1995 *National Headliner Award*. In 1999 he was a finalist for the *Pulitzer Prize*.

Rogers has also been the curator of two national cartoon exhibitions, *Too Hot to Handle: Creating Controversy through Political Cartoons* at The Andy Warhol Museum and *Bush Leaguers: Cartoonists Take on the White House* at the American University Museum.

He is currently serving as board president of the ToonSeum, a cartoon museum in Pittsburgh, Pennsylvania.